The Secret Door

To Mary

Gordon Greenall

The Secret Door

Gordon Greenall

First Published 2010

Line Drawings: Virginia and Lizzie Sandbach

Editing and proofreading: Maureen Morris

Published by Gordon Greenall Associates
4 Park Road, Chipping Campden, Gloucestershire, GL55 6EA

Printed in England by J F Print Limited, Sparkford

ISBN 978-0-9565242-0-1

Introduction to Linc

Leukaemia and Intensive Chemotherapy Fund

Only once (so far) have I been to talk to the Linc Charity, yet so much was I able to learn then about its manifold activities. A few years ago I was invited by a national newspaper to submit my most memorable couplet in English Literature, and I chose two lines from A. E. Housman:

And I will friend you, if I may,
In the dark and cloudy day.

Yes, that's what we all need in those cloudy days, and that's what Linc is: a friend to help – and to help hugely – when any of us is faced with the daunting and frequently frightening sequence of (take your pick!) cancer diagnosis, surgery, chemotherapy, radiotherapy, hospitalization, financial hardship, psychological distress… Alas, the list can be endless.

But what a combination of services Linc brings to cancer-sufferers! A selection (take your pick!) of medical expertise, intensive treatment, experienced care, practical assistance, psychological support, financial help… What else? Oh yes! Devoted patience and love.

I feel proud to be associated with this wonderful worthwhile charity.

Colin Dexter

Contents

Advice from the Owl

"Woo her" –
Coo's the owl
"Court her
Cavort with her -
Lift her from the page
Before she's caged
By the bars of old age.
Let her curves invite you -
Don't allow doubt
To spite you.
Throw out your arms –
Draw her towards you -
So close
Let her touch delight you.
Touch and caress
Squeeze - gently press
Her charms
Without hinder or qualms -
Walk with her
Talk to her –
Look into her mind –
But don't be swayed
By what you might find.
For she is a mystery
Beyond man's thoughts
As he courts her –
Cavorts her
With only advice
From his sage -
Between him
And old age."

Before Capture

We waved – we wished –
We wandered in the hollow mist
Of a silvered sapling morning
Whetted with a dry frost warning –
Throwing our voices with small concern
Against echo's sure return -
While drawn to tangle our unbound play
Against the spiders net display.

Pure pantomime set in a time
Of sibling play and distant crime -
Of innocence without care or cause to roam
More than a supper's distance slip from home -
To fish for spotted golden newts, dotted green frogs
And harmless snakes desperate for a hide of fallen logs
Or salt washed stones
Under which to rest their elastic bones.

How the sweet grass has soured now -
Black soil turned from rich beneath the plough
Where chasing crows once plucked grubs
From the tongues of untrained cubs
Throwing their, still thin screeches
Out, to fall before full height or reach
Could justly bandy grief
To each perching - lurching - wormy thief.

A time beneath drab slates of roofing cloud
Where we charged each particle of gain aloud
To slip across the rolling ground
As if in a pleasure, forever bound
In dilatory ponderings –
Dressed to suit our free of ration wanderings
Towards adventures dusted down of fear -
Born in the shade of a bright idea.

A splay of self-playing piano keys
Bouncing rhythmically to avoid a stray with fleas
Before capture turned our white keys black
And bent, into a rib and furrow back.
Bankrupt now are we once braves of pebble dash -
Authors of heroic deeds and gravel rash -
A willing - under shilling few that largess forgot
While lost in the pay of joy and tommy rot.

A Matter of Education

I would like to write a play
About a school of great renown -
Where each member of the staff
Was obliged to wear a gown
And the pupils – they were encouraged
To become more than a bunch of minions.
So I think I would name my school
St Catharine's or – (more probably) - St Trinian's.

Casting could be a problem though -
I'd have to ask my friends
Confessing – there'd be no wages paid -
They'd have to play for higher ends.
Such as the pleasure of performance -
And then of course there is the attraction -
That comes with so much
Uninhibiting - human interaction.

I would invite Marge
To take on the roll of Head
Knowing how well she would do -
Being – as she is indeed – so well read.
With Cathy as reverend Mother
Or perhaps to play the part of Matron -
One job being paired off with the other.

Geoff would hopefully play the part
Of Ron - the senior science master -
But have nothing to do with sport
To avoid a gym disaster.
Molly would be cast as
A (fearsome) Ofsted inspector
Who's report (while full and frank)
Would remain a matter for conjecture.

I see Nimi as Mini the Minx
Virginia as Beryl the Peril -
And Sue would be mistress of English Lit
In the guise of the writer Elizabeth Merril.
Lucy and Lynn
Would bounce in as new girls
In (extremely tight) navy skirts
With straw boaters askew on their pony-tailed curls.

The Head would promote Beryl - Head Girl -
A decision she might come to regret -
Because of Beryl's past misdemeanours
One school record the Head could never forget.
For the Head saw reputation as paramount
Which is why she politely rejected -
Beryl's offer to help with the new girls -
Even at the risk of them being neglected.

Matron would be the obvious choice
But she'd caused havoc in last year's school play -
By turning Dick Whittington into a farce
When the cat (she acquired) - ran away.
Besides there was the English teacher -
The demure (scholastic) Miss Merril -
Whom the Head felt sure would be a safe choice
To stop the new girls - turning feral.

Yes! Miss Merril was the obvious choice
As the Head had turned down an earlier offer from Ron
When he volunteered to - (Single-handedly)
Take on the duty of – "bringing the new girls on."
She had also discounted that minx – Mini
Though she first felt Mini could have taken the part
Until she read Mini's letter to the OFSTED inspector
The contents of which nearly stopped the Head's heart.

Mini's letter to the OFSTED inspector
Began - "Good golly, are you really Miss Molly?"
And went on to invite her to a midnight dorm party
Saying, "Bring your own weed and we'll all get jolly."
Going on to say, "We're not into book learning
Far more into good healthy sport
Though I'm into science - ask Ron what I do to his chemistry."
Now the Head's worried in case
Molly writes any of this down - in her OFSTED report.

Answering

I called you on the telephone.
A recorded voice, in monotone
Tells me there is no one home
So leave a message at the tone.
I leave a tape recorded groan,
And as I'm forced to postpone
I rage towards that answer tone
Conjoined to her telephone.

Text alerts with bells and chimes
Reminiscent of children's rhymes.
Annoying many ageing minds
Long past old folks' sleeping times.
Causing bad vibration textures
By going off while at the pictures,
Inside grounds at football fixtures,
Souring the best of cocktail mixtures.

Catching phrases, "How are you?"
"I'm still here, at the zoo."
"Yes, it's half past two."
"I can see a kangaroo."
Conversations on babies' dimples,
School children's pimples,
Nuns no longer wearing wimples
And! paranoid women's wrinkles.

I hear conversations
Spoke in language cultivations
By people outside railway stations
With radioactive imaginations -
About dog's homes closing down -
The state of London's Underground -
A naked red nosed, circus clown
Whose clothes weren't ever found.

I'd like to put each charging socket
In a safe and then forever lock it -
Fire a 'battery flattening' rocket
At every (phone infested) pocket.
And finally - I hope I might
Have a chance to put things right
By bringing to an end the flight
Of that damned communication satellite.

Away Day (New Street)

I stepped from the train onto Moor Street Station
And straight into the heart of a different nation.
There were girls wearing a variety of veils
Displaying the polish on their brightly coloured nails
And a youth had painted himself (blue) for a part
In a production of miming city street art.

A man waved a copy of the Bible about
Whilst ignoring the insults from an unpleasant lout.
The Community Bobbies looked clearly amused
As they consoled a Villa fan - apparently bemused
At having just heard the latest - terrible news
That they'd lost again - down at the Blues.

There was a busker strumming near to public seats
Being cursed by a man who was sweeping up the streets -
While a wheelchair athlete went flashing by
A mother taking grit from her little boy's eye -
All happening below a televised weather forecaster
Warning us all of an imminent flooding disaster.

There were men who called out that they wished you
Would take a free copy of the latest Big Issue -
Mostly ignored by the pre-occupied throng
Who seemed hell bent on simply rushing along -
But to where I just couldn't say -
I was far too busy keeping out of their way.

In front of a bank offering a wealth of fiscal advice -
Near to a shop selling suits below half of their original price
Paced a scruffy young man stuck to a red mobile phone
Who quickly changed from a conciliatory tone
To embark on a prolonged and abusive tirade
On the subject of benefits that he felt he hadn't been paid.

My intentions were to make my way up to Victoria Square
But I couldn't find anyone who knew the way there.
One man said go left while another insisted it was off to the right
The debate was so heated I was afraid they might start a fight -
So I went back to the station as it started to rain
And scrambled quickly aboard - the next homeward bound train.

Oh to Banish Broad Beans

Cabbage causes me sore spots
And sprouts give me the trots -
Macaroni tastes like bagging string
While curry brings a reddened ring.

Porridge gets right on my wick -
Semolina simply makes me sick -
While beetroot is a food I dread -
Staining my water a deathly red.

Runner beans I admit I like a lot
With gravy - served up piping hot
Poured over lamb with mint sauce -
And roasties - and fresh peas of course.

Though the beans I think I like the most
Are baked ones served on buttered toast -
With two farmyard eggs - lightly fried
And a grilled pork sausage on the side.

But those beans just known as broads,
To me - are simply black eyed frauds,
They are certainly the ones I loathe -
Though good for weaning pigs - I s'pose.

Bearing Trees

Those 'bearing trees' bear nothing now – their vacant bow
Clear from arc to squirrel's dray -
No fruit – no speckled eggs -
No canopy of leaves.

A compromise of purple dashed with slate - dormant twigs
Forming a disordered high border -
A loose – saw-tooth defence.

Rueing - retching – a redundant file of gnarled old guards
Above the barren orange clay -
No maize – no wheat -
No barley sheaves.

Winter has – with seedy coat of brick and brack let decay
Drop a curtain over autumn's order
And December 'cross her fence.

Bearing trees - seed high born – now dropped low – forlorn
In still pilgrimage – caught waiting
For fruit – for speckled eggs
For canopy of leaves.

Beyond the End of Day

I'd like to go beyond the end of day
Where (strange) sunset rainbows
Of orange – pink and magenta mauve
Striate through a smoking blue,
Thickening and darkening to a dull navy hue -
Hold sway -
Before night cowls all below - a shade of coal grey.

To become winged – free from gravity -
Be drawn into colourful hospitality
Where my thoughts would be brightly lit
And layered in the moist, mellow
Light complexions, from a golden yellow –
Venerated orb
Of wisdom – that I might (in part) absorb.

Suddenly – my thoughts are interrupted
By a fleeting - pinkened skein of geese -
Distant heralds, calling time
Along the high edge of a tumbling day -
Their beating wings folding away
The last brittle rays of twilight -
(Hid from sight)
Raising the plight of low nocturnal prey.

So - as I dream of the waiting to learn my worth
From (extra terrestrial) translucent scribes -
Cloaked in ivory and aquamarine
Over tabards of aubergine-green -
The drip of night blocks all - falling first -
Turning black from bad to worse -
Mummifying
The slow turning – dark cooling – wild-blue earth.

Biking to Work

Sometimes I look back to the days of my youth,
When punishment for lying was confused with the truth,
And in order that you didn't grow up a young fool
They'd put you to work long before school.
I can see galvanised buckets and hessian sacks
For young mothers - all bending their backs,
To fill them to bulging with potatoes to mash
Or to boil or to roast, or to turn into much needed cash.

I was given an old bike coloured in black and in rust:
It was the sort of bike you knew you could trust;
A bike that could talk as I travelled along,
It's squeaking and groaning was just like a song.
But as I peddled to work I heard my bike moan:
If you travel with me you don't travel alone;
Even when you travel back to your home,
If you travel with me then you don't travel alone.

Many evenings were spent with paper sacks full,
Delivering the news - through fine weather and dull.
While alone - except for my bike coloured rusty and black,
And hundredweights of news compressing my back
I'd think of some changes I'd like to make,
Not just for me, but for everyone's sake.
I'd fill in the potholes that caused all those spills
And while I was about it, I'd iron out the hills.

Some times my black bike coloured with rust
Spent part of the day just gathering dust -
As I bent my back double digging the veg -
Or top of a ladder, clipping the hedge.
Pushing a mower, cutting the lawn -
A job I did best just after dawn -
For Miss Moody, a lady of local renown
And for Miss Tomlinson's whole half-a-crown.

My rusty black bike took me to school,
Till that one day when I acted the fool,
By giving three lads a lift after gym
I believe they were called Trevor, Robert and Tim.
Mr Jones, made it clear he wasn't amused
At the way my old bike had been so badly abused,
So I did detention with the French teacher's wife
And my bike - it was banned for the rest of my life.

Blaster Bronc

The quarryman's whistling
Would pierce the winter dark,
Travellin' well in front of 'im,
And competing with the lark.
It drowned out the squeakin'
From 'is rusty cotter pin
An' put the vicar off performin'
Yet another mortal sin.

Now 'e was known as Bronc
By 'is fellow quarrymen
Cos 'e seemed well suited
To life - in a donkey pen.
But I thinks this be unfair
Cos 'e was much younger when
'E slipped up with a hairy mare,
E's calmed down a lot since then.

Ol' Bronc 'e took the lid off
A box with sticks o' dynamite.
But when 'e looked inside
'E saw a very sorry sight.
The box 'ad bin in the rain
An' all the sticks was damp.
They wouldn't blow yer 't off,
Nor wake a sleepin' tramp.

Bronc put the box inside the office
To dry out by the fire grate.
Well them sticks became quite active
By dryin', at a very rapid rate.
The explosion took the roof off,
Sendin' the winders flyin' wide
An' set fire to the chimney,
With the foreman still inside.

They called a short enquiry
To determine what went wrong.
Ol' Bronc said it was clear
That the office it 'ad gone.
But there was a bit o' good news
'Cus the dynamite 'ad dried out well,
An' the foreman wasn't comin' back,
Or so that's what 'e'd 'eard tell.

Next week ol Bronc 'ad put
Explosives into the quarry face.
'E lit the fuses from 'is brier pipe
Then smoked it somewhere safe.
But Bronc 'ad put too much powder in
An' the face went on to overload,
Which soon became apparent-
When some fallout - landed in the road.

Some clattered into the bed
Of a returnin' tipper lorry.
The driver said "this is the quickest
I've ever bin, loaded in this quarry".
Yet more of the lime stun landed
On top of a foreign tourist bus -
Causin' them ruddy Germans
To kick up a mighty fuss.

Then some of the stun - fell onto
The foreman's 'orse drawn hearse.
Well, this was a bit embarrassing
But it could 'ave bin much worse.
Although it smashed the coffin
An' 'is top 'at - with a mighty force -
All them chunks of flyin' stun,
Completely missed the 'orse.

The foreman could be in 'eaven
Accordin' to a medium's message -
Just as Ol' Bronc went off to Oz'
On a ten pound assisted passage.
So as to carry on is quarry work -
Which filled them outback folk with fear.
I wonder if that's the reason why -
There's so many on 'em - over 'ere.

Blonde and Booted

It was there upon the sofa
Where this sight I spied
There they were crossed legged -
And booted side by side.
Boots brown - tightly laced
Stretching to the knees
Boots buff - laced wide and loosely
Worn, it seemed with ease.

Though laces brown were flat
Buff were clearly round
All tied on boots that crossed
Those boots firmly on the ground -
Containing two legs clad in denim
All women could afford,
While two were tightly wrapped
In a finely woven cord.

What goes on above those boots
Is a mystery - more or less
Beyond the minds of men, at which I -
For one, wouldn't like to even guess.
Can I hear a cackling?
Or just the dizzy heights of chatter -
Should I try to understand?
Or simply disregard the matter.

So boots brown - boots buff
I choose not to raise
My thoughts above the knee -
But rest my gaze
On those calves of suede -
Knowing I may never persuade
Them - even to try to satisfy
A curious mind -
Left behind – to wonder why.

Dropped Nuts

Peanuts – tied - caged –
Hung out as bait
For early rising birds
As well as those arriving late.

Hard – cold – high
Hung with holes too small
To abate the hunger
Felt by each and all.

Tit – robin – finch
Flying to and fro -
Bullied into dropping nuts -
To appease - the vengeful crow.

Melting Ice and Liquid Snow

But still they could not cross the mighty river flow
For her banks had spread in awesome flood
Swelled by tides of melting ice and liquid snow.

Paddle boats set out to cut the swell and mow
As large as heads of steam and revolutions could
But still they could not cross the mighty river flow.

Though men sat at bow and stern in pairs to power row
They could not reach across that span in craft of wood
Swelled by tides of melting ice and liquid snow.

They sat to wait till storm would drop her blow
But she did not - to leave them knowing that they should
But still they could not cross the mighty river flow.

They must seek the ferry chain a dozen feet below
In hope to pull their way across the flood for good
Swelled by tides of melting ice and liquid snow.

It was their last gasp draw to cross the Ohio
They pulled so hard- that some shed life and blood
But still they could not cross the mighty river flow
Swelled by tides of melting ice and liquid snow.

Boyhood Sacrifice

I remember a boyhood of sacrifice made
Before winter sports could be played -
Of the indignities born
With all those clothes that had to be worn -
To keep us wrapped up – snug and warm
And safe - from general harm -
Before being let out to play
With the (added) warning – 'not to stray'.

Then sacrificing some of my calm
At the thought of meeting 'General Harm'-
Whom - I assumed had platoons
Of light dragoons - on the go
Quick marching - or strutting out slow -
Over the lay of my personal snow -

Accompanied by husky dog sledges
Ripping over snow buried hedges -
Before drifting askew
All over my - white world tattoo –
Until I would find
All those dogs were only whelped - in my mind –
So I had to yield
To the truth - that the only dog - out in the field
Was a spaniel
I nicknamed Daniel -
Embroidered onto my red woollen scarf -
Without a throat to growl or to bark.

So - darkness falls -
As far as I can recall –
With Daniel and I
Going home - to a plate of leftovers pie
Followed by jam roly poly for pud –
Though Daniels appetite's not very good –
He's just not in the mood -
Having been put off his food
By the lack of good hedges
And all those (sore throated) dogs - pulling sledges.

Bric-a-brac

They pour in through the open doors
Those anoraks and collecting bores -
Earnest in their garbled talk
About the merits of a pickle fork,
Pre-war compacts by Max Factor
And a wheel from a Fordson tractor,
While two women - wearing woolly hats
Fall out about some china cats.

Stock displayed on tables under racks
Of dog-eared well-read paper-backs,
1950's Beano comic annuals
And a pile of MG sports car manuals.
A Mrs. Beeton's household book
Has a page marked with a button-hook,
Hallmarked - Chester 1882 -
Once servant to a lady's shoe.

Some sixties Matchbox toys
Once the joy of all small boys
Have grown up a bit since then
Into collector's toys for ageing men.
A one-armed man upsets his wife
By buying a sharp-edged Ghurka knife.
She scolds "You're as batty as an owl -
Far better off with garden trowel."

A buyer of ladies underwear
Waves a fifties basque with a little tear
Before offering a fist full of Euro bills
For a pile of linen laced with frills -
Just as she's hit by a speeding wheelchair
Driven by a bloke without due care –
Who roars displeasure, before she can say,
"I'm awfully sorry if I was in your way."

The refreshment room is serving pies
To women dressed like Russian spies
Who stand around in hushed debate
About a girl who's lately put on weight.
While they eat the last of the carrot cake
To the disgust of a man with a garden rake -
A girl with auburn hair and a teddy bear
And a collector of 1930's Carlton-ware.

A deal is done with a Danish stoker
By an elfin-like habitual smoker
Before she wraps a book she intends to lend
To a hyper-chatty Scottish friend,
Who has already sent a text to state,
That she's delayed and will be late,
Because the car won't start that she'd hoped to sell
And what's more the cat's not well.

The crowds diminish as it starts to snow
Which puts a damper on the show.
So the dealers pack away each stall
To avoid being stranded at the hall
Then an ageing man is heard to shout
"There's a package burning - put it out."
Suspicion falls on a smoker who
Screams, "My God - What shall I do."

The fire's doused from a biscuit tin
By a portly bloke with a tight lipped grin.
Just as the Scottish friend arrives at last
And relates the woes of her recent past.
The elfin smoker suggests that they should take
A well-earned tea or coffee break -
As she grabs for the contraband in her bag
For the rewarding taste of one last fag.

The two girls find a pair of vacant chairs
Next to some chattering friends of theirs.
Fortunately seated at some smoking tables
Set in booths below grey plastic gables.
The waitress says there'll be quite a wait.
To which the smiling elf says "Great -
Because I've no desire to hurry back
To a draughty hall piled high with bric-a-brac".

Brush of Words

Pensmith! - rouse those so immature -
Small of opinion - uninformed - insecure.
Splash them with words that take the fore
And stir view point's cauldron all the more.

Spill discordant thoughts - like condiments
Sniffed into the minds of malcontents -
Spread a feathered touch of enlightenment
To soften their (coarse-brushed) argument.

Ameliorate those drab ingrates
With views not served to discriminate -
But reiterate - regenerate – illuminate
And whet illusion's wit for fresh debate.

Free vermilion - copper - violet and sage
From the bastion of their bunkered cage -
Let alabaster - indigo – green and beige
Cast new rainbows over written page.

Oh wordsmith bring about an illustrated spate
Of painted thoughts on which to contemplate
Such signs that show how history does dictate -
Through her penned words - all future's fate.

Oh poet - take your brush of words and paint
To show those shackled by constraint
Or hindered by a voice of mal-informed complaint -
An overview of life - without restraint.

Calmed - the Prussian Wind

If no Fascist Prussian fringe -
Then no hellish plans
To build extermination camps-
Where skulls would lie attached
By only a single - sinew thread
To bones – unbleached –
Un-maintained - just stained in blood
To be heaped – abandoned -
As though only fuel - to feed the burning flood.

No sunken empty sockets
Staring – sightless -
Like demonic gargoyles
Brought crashing down to bedlam
As though felled by cannon –
Blown from God's enlightenment
To an abject misery
By hands proudly dressed
In their master's (deaths head) livery.

No deserted – stark corpses
Gone – burnt – destroyed.
No victim's bile would – in purgatory -
Haunt those, bearing unseeing, uncaring witness.
Those - who would not have need of ill spleen
Nor to turn their backs on victims
Dead and yet un-dead -
And would have no need to claim 'they only followed
Where the jack-boot led'.

Frost warning

At twenty to four this morning
Cold winter oozed in from the dark
Through window - ajar – no warning
At twenty to four this morning
Rime frost on the apple – adorning
My garden – before the clear lark
At twenty to four this morning
Cold winter oozed in from the dark.

Campden Town FC

From fields on farms to council recreation grounds
A home for her was sought and found
Where young men could gather round and play
Unhindered – under rules – on a winter's day.
Donning shirts once black and gold
Across the years grown ripped and old -
Bleached out in wash tubs to a faded grey
But still donned with pride - from opening day till into May.
Witnessed by men who leant their bikes on silver trees
And stood in baggy caps and baggy trousered knees
To cheer or boo - or moan just as they please
While tireless ladies busied, making teas.
But the cheers and groans - the constant roar
That came with goals and fouls - are heard no more.

The posts are down
The nets are gone
The lines there faded
The grass is long.
Alf has died
His last collection done -
The old club is nil
Lack of interest won.
No more games
Nor fixture dates
So the playing field
Is left to fate -
With a notice saying
'You're here too late
So last man out
Please close the gate.'

Only echoes sound now of those who once played –
Played the game for health and recreation -
For comradeship, team spirit and through single minded effort -
Found virtue in striving for and achieving success
And the purity gained from halcyon endeavour.
Now only dog walkers and directionless youths
Linger where such memorable heroics once took place.
Lets us hope that team spirit only slumbers
And not - as feared – is dashed for ever.

Afternoon Reading

The shrill urgency of the ward slowed
Around two-o-clock
To a low hush - almost to a full stop
As we small boys
Sat cross-legged and fairly hypnotised
By the wonders
Of animated freshwater mystery
That streamed from Nurse Neatly's warm voice
As she read aloud
Another episode from 'the book of our choice'.

She would make Mole, Ratty and Toad come alive -
With their plans and their schemes
Becoming part of our dreams -
While we were refreshed by 'The Wind in the Willows',
Her colleagues made up our beds
With the whitest of sheets
And crispest of covers slipped over our pillows.

As she read on - the vacuum cleaner arrived
With such a noise
It quickly distracted the most attentive of boys.
Just as the evidence
Was to be read out against Toad
The vacuum roared out -
In a vacuous language we took to be code.

By the time that peace was restored
And we boy's re-absorbed
Toad's escape plans had already been carefully laid
And helped by his friends
His bold dash for freedom successfully made.
I remember thinking
That by now they could be eating and drinking
Home baked fruit cake and fresh lemonade.

But I couldn't be sure of any of this -
Unable to work out how it had all come about -
Rendered no doubt,
By the vacuum's repetitive whir, into a forty-winks bliss.
So this mystery
Would just have to wait till I was at least seven or eight
Having by then, learnt to read
And reach the boys' shelf,
Take down the book and find out for myself.

Careless Cloud

That careless cloud of morning rain
Poured her random pain
Round the rim of Conduit Hill
Across the scarp to Dyer's Lane –
Soaking (already) sodden ground
Found spread – to re-arrange the Hoo
Into water-logged high rise bogs
And overflow her cruel brown stew.

So the westerly cauldron tipped
Her indiscriminate swell
Out across the mildewed crops
To bring Park Road a liquid hell
Of amorphous atropine
Swelling the brown turmoil
Come on effluent's calling card -
To soil with her own foul spoil.

Her hidden teeth (exposed) snatched
The leaf from a peaceful dove -
Drew blood from a concrete hand
Through its tarmacadam glove.
While her claws tore at the Cotswold walls -
Pushed in the bursting doors
And dragged the sodden spoil out -
From a street of sobbing floors.

Gaunt sunken eyes spoke no lies
As they looked on in despair -
Soaking in their pleas for help
(As at last) some began to gather there -
To turn about old memories -
Churned out in fractured ware
Onto Littleworth's (unlit) pyre
By near neighbours – doused with care.

Boiling rage sated - disaster done
The invader subsides - slinking away
Past un-sleeping - un-noticing exhaustion -
Without further reason left to stay -
Leaving young, old, ill and well
Seemingly sealed in a mean quiet tomb
Gathering - consoling – preparing
To start – the long march from that cloud of doom.

Charlie's Water Otter

Mr Pyment walked from 'ome
To Charlie Ladbrook's, that wasn't very far –
An' once in Charlie's passage
'e found the kitchen door ajar –
'e called out to Charlie loudly
To draw 'im from the front room fire
Sayin' "I must speak to you –
Before time calls you to retire."

"Retire!" exclaims Ol' Charlie –
"No I'm not that old yet."
"I simply meant to bed for the night –
I knew this call I would regret" –
Mr Pyment sighed.
"Before I left home, I said
I need to talk to Charlie about his rampant weeds -
But hope that when I call – he's already gone to bed."

"Now what be you a referrin' to."
Charlie said, "I have no weeds –
Me garden's filled with rare an' exotic flora
Grown from very costly seeds –
That's why I have them 'Lightfoot' 'ens -
A quite specialised an' costly breed
That treads over me garden all delicate like -
In a way they wouldn't bother - if it was only full of weeds."

"I think you'll find they are Light Sussex."
Mr Pyment moaned.
"No," said Charlie, "They comes from Lighthorn 'eath."
Mr Pyment groaned.
"I'm not hear to discus your poultry –
It's my yard - where your 'exotic flora' are seen spilling."
"Well now you'm in luck," said Charlie,
"Cos they'm free – no charge - not even 'alf a shillin'."

Mr Pyment drew a deeper breath
And sighed - as his sight an' 'earin' came t' fuse
Was there ever such an annoying man –
And if so - I hope he's never found – He then went on to muse.
As his senses cleared –he looked Charlie in the eyes –
Which wasn't very wise – and then was heard to shout –
"I'm sending my two yardmen round
To clear my yard and your hedgerow out."

"Tis a garden wall," said Charlie - dolefully -
"It's all that straggling' undergrowth you know
That stops them bricks an' mortar
From a puttin' on - a proper wallin' show."
Mr Pyment turned to the door – then implored,
"And try and tidy up - your side of the blocked up brook."
Charlie sighs and says, " My rheumatics be a playin' up" -
But at least 'e then promised - 'e would take a look.

A few days later Charlie 'appened to be passin'
By the blocked up brook –
An' so felt obliged (by 'is promise)
To at least stop an' take a look.
'is interest was taken by all the rubbish
That 'ad come from near an' far
To block the brook – as some was merely scrap
But some was - to ol' Charlie - object d'art.

Then 'e spots somethin' very rare
An' steps lively t' the Lion
An' tells all drinkin' there, "Somethin's in the brook
That you fellas should cast your eye on.
Quickly now - leave your cider pots
Make 'aste an' come with me
For tis a rare an' fancy water otter
As you will plainly see."

Timmy Brotheridge gets knocked sideways
But Ernie Lockyear 'elps 'im up –
For Timmy 'ad lost 'is balance
A tryin' not t' spill 'is cider cup.
Finally - Timmy manages t' get a look
An' sez, "That is no otter though it 'as a shiny skin.
It 'as no snout just a dented spout
An' I'm sure it's made of tin."

Then Charlie starts t' snigger as 'e sez
"It's what I told you - as it's bin used for 'ottin' water
Till it was recklessly thrown out
By that there solicitor's flighty daughter."
But those gathered there was not best pleased
At Charlie's bit of fun
An' the way that they reacted
Caused ol' Charlie - t' turn on 'is 'eals - an' run.

The Cherub and Tyke

A soft breeze ruffles
The twigs of the larch
As its warm meanderings
Turns from crawl into march
On the grey (dispirited) snow
Hanging about now -
Like putrefied clusters
Of fruit browned on the bough.

Bare ruts of tarmac -
Verges and well wintered soil -
All are besmirched by
Irregular shrinkings of spoil
Simply hanging around -
Lounging in pockets of shade
To some extent cast there
By a vigorous shovel parade.

An unwanted midden
Of off-white sharps and flats
Scaled and conquered by
Minxes and brats -
Drawn together in ardour
And dressed so alike -
They become indistinguishable -
Twins now - as cherub and tyke.

Cherubs and tykes – (enraptured) -
In bright yellow and orange cagoules
Pink cheeks the brighter
For days - spent out of school
High on blanched pastures -
Above frozen streams
Where (one time) minxes and brats
Slip merrily - through wonderland dreams.

From their (all too) brief plummetings
The minxes and brats invite
Their parents to take part in
Their childlike delight -
By casting off cares
As were the pram - trike and bike
And ride the fleeced cloud of innocence
With (all too) fleeting - cherub and tyke.

Cold Room

Once vibrant room blown warm
By urgent words
And pointless chatter -
Absorbed into her walls
As might blind toxic fall out
Be - from rays of gamma matter.

But now she knows no variance
In sighs of love
Or barking violence
That echoed then on her
(Horsehair) limed clay walls -
Too long caged in bars of silence.

Her pores (cold) sweat damp slime -
Conjoining rooms
Cast to be part house -
Drip dropped spawlings
To spatter spore rotted floor -
And douse the fleeing wood-louse.

Ceiling lathe exposed – hopelessly
Pinned by sprigs
Of ragged oxidation
To tusk-tenoned trimmer
Adzed naked of rough bark -
Charred by (bygone) conflagration.

Bisque imprinted – broken bricks -
Half name done
Co. Ltd. Long gone
Fall on bruised lank floor
Bringing waney elm to creek -
Splitting – shaking – twisting - wan.

At flint hearth a brick leeched void
Lets Priest Hole
Whisper (hiss) of gold
To opportunist trencherman -
With a cloak of magnolia bones
Grasping a loose rolled sepia scroll.

Conversation with the Pavement

As I walked slowly, tread by weary tread,
Along the painful way ahead
The pavement spoke in resonation,
"Don't stamp your feet with such a beat
You bring too loud an echo
To my asphalt marl concrete."

My introspection saw blisters too -
Sore - split and chapping aggregate,
Chipped and worn out shale - no doubt
Caused by travellers running late.

A new surface – laid by the yard,
Replaces long worn cobbled stone
To help deaden - with crepe-soled shoe -
This ancient stretch of 'tramping' zone,

That had wended there in war and peace
Through pestilence - famine and rare feast,
And felt the shod and cloven hooves
Of many a market driven beast.

Felt the hobbling cobbler's gout -
The weight of fair day stalls
And reverberated to the iron hoop -
Rolled into her stone walls.

By now I breathed more slowly -
Caught by the cotton frost.
"Was future mine – or his?" The pavement asked -
I - now in frantic panic – feel quite lost.

"The way is yours – not mine."
I came to call, in time.
"My sore heels must rest their beat.
While you are still trod by urgent feet,
Feet that beat to your tune -
Upon your asphalt - marl concrete."

Daffodils and Mint

As daffodil bells ring in fat lambs
Each burgeoning March and April
Some the weight of boneless hams
As daffodil bells ring in fat lambs -
Eaten with mint jellies and jams
Till diners have taken their fill -
As daffodil bells ring in fat lambs -
Each burgeoning March and April.

Fog Bound

Beneath a quilt of grey morning cloud -
Cloaking a frost coated brier hedge
A pheasant cock called out aloud
Beneath a quilt of grey morning cloud
Dropped down like an errant shroud
To mask high tree and low water's edge
Beneath a quilt of grey morning cloud -
Cloaking a frost coated brier hedge.

Course Bridge

After dark they park their cars
In winter streets devoid of stars
The door opens as the bell is rung
They enter in - their coats are hung
Or draped on rails by the stairs
Or over backs of wooden chairs.
Time to sit with drink and talk about
Their day - until the cards come out.

The ribald chatter now is muffled
As the red pack's out and being shuffled
Expectant pleasure now is felt
As one by one the cards are dealt.
Thirteen to each one of the four
Who sort their hands and count their score.
Then the dealer opens as he starts
With a bid of 'one in hearts'.

"Course Bridge," is called by South
When East cannot control his mouth.
West calls a hand of spades but as he speaks
His smile confirms it is his best for weeks.
South glowers at the way the bidding starts
And then comes in with three in hearts
While North shows he is clearly troubled
As they are - by West - now firmly doubled.

East displays a hint of furtiveness
That suggests four clubs is just finesse
But North is pleased the double's off
Which clearly shows in his nervous cough.
West decides 'no bids' the call,
While South preys hard that East will fall
For she sees her clubs are long
And with high spades her hand is strong.

North leads diamonds - a suit not called at all
West plays the five - a card that's far too small -
While South trumps in with such a pace
It takes the trick from East with waiting ace.
The tension that was slight begins to mount
As each pair checks the others count,
Till East concedes - which is the sign
For South - to record her score above the line.

Glasses chink as drinks are poured
Totals rise as points are scored.
So the night wears on to way past ten
Before the rubber ends and play begins again.
The call is hearts the contract's red
With South declaring she would rather be in bed,
Then roars with anger on her face,
When East calls out, "I know who has the ace."

Tetchy hands by all are played
Until the winning contract's made.
While the cards are packed away once more
South spies an ace upon the floor.
"It was dropped by you, you beast,"
She screams towards the startled East.
North then leaves with West and some dread,
As South and East go up to bed.

Costly Discharge

Belched out smoke which bests the cut
And counteracts hoar winter frost
Specked with blowing pinhead smut
Belched out smoke which bests the cut
But not the price with heated soot
Each pennyweight caught as the cost
Belched out smoke which bests the cut
And counteracts hoar winter frost.

Cross Country Joy

As a cross-country run turns into a pleasant jog
Perhaps little more than a Wednesday roam -
To some even worth all the sinew straining slog
Just to know the joy felt when sighting home.

Perhaps little more than a Wednesday roam -
An excursion each boy's been keen to book
Just to know the joy felt when sighting home
Around the bend in Basket Weaver's Brook.

An excursion each boy's been keen to book -
In exchange for maths he will be running free
Around the bend in Basket Weaver's Brook -
To return to fresh cut cake and hot mug of tea.

In exchange for maths he will be running free
To skip across those miles of undulating pasture
To return to fresh cut cake and hot mug of tea -
Just as an elder brother did in winning last year.

To skip across those miles of undulating pasture
Is a great experience – for those running to enjoy
Just as an elder brother did in winning last year -
While building strength into the adolescent boy.

Is a great experience - for those running to enjoy -
An event to be endured with fortitude and grace -
While building strength into the adolescent boy
For such joy will not be felt in any other race.

An event to be endured with fortitude and grace
To some even worth all the sinew straining slog
For such joy will not be felt in any other race -
As a cross-country run turns into a pleasant jog.

Hard Crusts

Hard crusts abandoned
To the mange and stubble lawn
Like fallen rhododendron leaves
Half scorched – half bleached –
Too dry to rot,
Too dense to leave
As airborne dross
On an early autumn breeze -
As though held - cast
Till damped by scattered rain
Or crushed by the rapier thrusts
From a landing of ravenous crows.

Sisters and Cats

Two sisters they where called upon
To feed the family cat
One would leave the household key
Hid beneath the outside mat.
But sister one is in a rush
To catch the London train
And dashes off - still with the key -
Along Broad Marston lane.

Later - sister two arrives
To do her duty to the family pet
But she can not entry gain
For the key is not there yet.
She rings around to summon help
And wants them all to know
That she is keyless - all alone -
Save for the red eyed crow.

Dark Thoughts

You caught him a very hard blow
I'm sure he'll die, if we leave him out here.
But nobody knows it was us
We'll get away with it, never you fear.

I still say we should take him to casualty
We could use my old van, it's not too far
But if we take him for treatment
We'll be seen - so they'll know who we are.

This is not about us - it's about him
And the very real threat to his life
Ah he won't be missed, he looks like a tramp
But he could have been on the way home to his wife.

I'm not risking prison for him
I'll bet if he has a wife they live in a shack
You can tell by his dark curly hair
And brown skin - look - he's definitely black.

But he's in a serious condition – and I am aware
That he's come here from a part of the commonwealth
Well there you are – you see - you agree
No! I'm simply concerned with the threat to his health.

You can do as you like I'm going home
If you want to be a hero – then do it alone
I'm not leaving him here that's for sure
If I have to - I'll take him there on my own.

OK we'll carry him to your van – then I'm gone -
Oh! And if there is a reward some for me would be fair.
You've always said you want no truck with the blacks
True – but if their money is being divied out
Then of course I still want my share!

December's Delight

Bright December afternoon
Sees the lowering distant sun
Cast a biscuit yellow light
To catch the pale feathers
Of the partridge's underwing -
On his frantic take-off flight.

Fly - all small sweeping game
From the spaniel keen in pace -
His black patchwork bounds
In step with off white back
Through long cover, high as he -
Wavering to his chasing rounds.

Low over dying barley's stubble
Go lengthening walkers' shadows.
Across green topped turnips deep -
Displaying their new fodder leaf
In striped and mottled arable,
Sown to graze dull winter's sheep.

The Sun paints with soft edged brush
Long ridge and furrow mounds,
To highlight their green and black -
Light and shade - long since husbanded -
Now come abandoned to be bound
Back - by fence from wayfare's track.

The scut of a startled rabbit doe
Bobs in tune to her confusion -
On her dash along the bridleway
In light and shade of shadows
Growing longer, stretching - taut -
Absorbed into the closing day.

So - amid this scene we tread
Our way from Lapstone edge
Along the ancient packhorse way -
Where once trod snorting mare
Or braying mule, wet and cold
Till 'well the other side of May'.

Each irregular step leading us
To the view of Broad Campden Vale
Spreading out her ancient wares
In a most unblemished welcome
As awaits the Baker's Arms
To wash away our blistered cares.

Her history now fully done
And long since written down
Gives hard evidence in lime
As shown in church and chapel -
Manor and each low – pale-lit home
Of a once - more humble time.

Old dog still pulling for joy
Past the elm - the Quaker home
And Maidenwell's manorial door
To skirt along the high path
Across Croft's field and brook
To return - fine in spirits more.

First Novelty Verse

The round stack put up at first
Caused a Cork farmer to curse
For he'd planned on a slim rick
Because it rhymed with Limerick
To create a new novelty verse.

A Means of Escape

I went to my car which was covered in frost
That I was unable to scrape off – to my cost
It seemed that my 'just cause' was finally lost
As I tossed away - my scraper of frost –
Becoming resigned - now that my cause was lost
And I could only hope to cope - at the most
To making my last gasp escape to the coast
As a written plea - perhaps only in boast -
Securely sealed – stamped and sent off in the post.
That's how - so sadly - I lost in my haste -
Any slim chance of making good my escape.

Any slim chance of making good my escape
Fell with those malicious false charges of rape
Made by a woman in a black woollen cape -
Waving a quite badly damaged video tape -
Well marked - with many a scratch and a scrape
And wrapped in a piece of sponge rubber crepe –
Bulging - rounded and bound out of shape.
Stuffed - dishonestly with scurrilous lies -
Like a dim lit room full of MI5 spies
Who claim that their intrigue and tenuous ties -
All are ingrained by Mossad - making them wise.

All are ingrained by Mossad - making them wise -
Giving them great power over life and demise -
Being God given – coming down from the skies
And covering all that crawls and that which flies –
Helping me not – as my various lame tries
To claim innocence - become blown away cries –
Which I find isn't really much of a surprise.
As I hurriedly try to plan my defence
With only facts and not a hint of pretence –
So I ask simply for small recompense
In my strongly worded attempt at defence.

In my strongly worded attempt at defence -
(That's formed in plain English and good common sense)
Bringing a lift to my morale – that's immense -
When the charges were dropped for the offence
Of which I was maliciously accused -
Leaving me full of joy - though a little bemused -
And more so as the garage mechanic - somewhat confused -
Was saying that my car was being misused -
And should – (in future) - be more properly used.
At this point my wires became somewhat fussed -
As once again I was unfairly accused.

As once again I was unfairly accused
I felt my ego being quite badly bruised –
In fact my whole being felt sorely contused
As I sat in the chair and quietly mused
Over the effects of a hard winter frost -
Of it's possible effects and grievous cost
To all the good living that I almost lost -
Because of a badly wrapped video tape
Poorly portraying an improbable rape
And twisting my battered wits so out of shape -
That I just panicked for a means of escape.

Glad to Have Him Be

On my way - by the graveyard
I was somewhat strangely
Drawn - through the open gate
To take a shorter route
And miss the teeming throng -
That would surely make me late.

Just then the sun burst through the trees
To fleck a quiet grave
Unkempt - kept overgrown
Where a father had lain - so long
His babbling offspring
Are - (by now) - all weaned and flown.

A large Norwegian spruce waved
Frenetically - to send her needles
Falling slowly on the breeze -
A breeze I heard whispering
Within my saddened mind - like spirits
Wheezing – caught beneath those towering trees.

Whispering - you were both of an age -
Together in your over-doings
As were all young men.
You knew him well enough -
Enough to think his thoughts
But know by now - you never shall again.

Those simple thoughts - spoken plainly -
Fitting in well with the rest of us –
Straightforward - sure – sane -
Glad to be - as we were glad
To have him be - in wit and thought -
But know well by now – we never shall again.

In memory of David Hobbs 1945 - 1973

A Letter to Marge

Dear Marge
I'm not sure what to do
So I'm writing to you
After all you are the person-in-charge.
This homework's such a difficult task
All about food that could be misconstrued
As rude - if not properly chewed
And I couldn't think of anyone else that I could ask.

By the way - I saw a woman eating bananas and ham -
Right there on her plate.
Such a strange mixture she ate -
Which brought the question what did she have with jam?
This turned my thoughts to my school days -
When food was on ration
And we ate 'after a fashion'-
For want of an alternative phrase.

In summer we were fed salads
Of greens and potatoes and meat -
Which didn't do at all well in the heat -
As recalled in one of our ballads
Worded thus – *The salad is fake –*
It's been made since the war
So don't go asking for more
'cause it will give your belly the ache.

Another song that we always sung
Was about stew and jam tart
But I can only remember the start -
Though there's a cow on the tip of my tongue.
My one dislike was rice pudding's skin crust
Which caused me to ask, "Miss -
Do I really have to eat this?"
To which she always replied "Yes you must."

The meat was always corned beef or spam
Which we carved into sheds
Or bald teacher's heads
And sometimes - the odd caravan -
Which, naturally was not very wise -
Because if the teachers caught us
There was a terrible fuss -
In which we were severely chastised.

Then there was Angus Webb's dislike of beetroot -
Which brought forth this plea -
"Believe me – it discolours your wee
And leaves a maroon stain on your boot."
Noddy Maycock – when faced with salad - just cried -
Believing lettuce had bugs
That grew into seven inch slugs
Who could eat their way out – from inside.

Strange what thoughts come to a man -
Just by watching Dorothy
Wash away with her tea
A plateful of bananas and ham.
And I'm still wondering if she's a lover of spam -
Ever dreamt of pork chops with custard
Or fruit cake with mustard -
But mostly – I'd like to know what she has with her jam.

P.S. I've just been told she had tea with the Vicar
Where she was elaborately fed
With pink spread on brown bread
While wearing an '**I was there**' sticker.
Well! I've since discovered she wasn't served
With the best of smoked salmon
Or thinly sliced gammon -
But crab apple jam – so her secret's no longer preserved.

Better with Jam

Supper time - what an array
The evening table set – at the end of a perfect day.
I couldn't choose between the cold lamb
And the fresh slices of ham –
One eaten with home made mint sauce –
The other with mustard – of course.
My thought pattern was then broken
By Gran - with this token –
They both taste much better - with jam.

Much Better with Jam

I went for a ride on a tram
With my new girlfriend Pam.
She offered me a sandwich of cheese
That dripped onto my knees
With the runniest of gooseberry jam.

I said to her, "Pam –
I know why we ride on this tram -
But could you explain to me please
Why there's preserve on my cheese."
To which she replied,
"They taste much better with jam."

Fingers in too many Pies

A giggle of nymphs and seraphs
Agreed to form a goblin troupe
And with a taste for fairy cakes
They joined a cookery group.
But the smallest nymph played truant
So she could fly her paper kite,
Until the day it flew away –
Competely out of sight.

The kite was soon spied, high
In a tree - up near the crown.
Aloft – to bring her kite back down.
But in her haste she rashly slipped
From that leafy beech-
Into the swirling frog spawn pool -
Away from wise owl's reach.

Though at first it seemed
That she had sadly gone
Her fall brought repercussions
While her ripples lingered on.
The class were now quite down
Without her noisy chatter there -
And no more cosmic recipes
For - those tiny cooks to share.

The wise old owl said "Nymph
The course is far too much I fear,
I know you've attended sometimes
But more often you're not here."
The nymph then slowly scrambled
Out from her tadpole hell
Then yelled "It doesn't bother me,
I'll do the Wednesday class as well."

With each Wednesday afternoon
The wood nymph's kudos grew
For she organised the students -
As well as vetting anybody new.
So the mid-week class became
A great culinary success
But meanwhile - the one she left
Had become a squabbling mess.

"Don't worry owl all will be fine",
Said nymph – (by woodland telegraph).
"I'll explain the rules to everyone,
Which I'm sure will bring a laugh."
But one or two misunderstood -
In a way the nymph had not supposed,
Manifested in the cookery riots -
So now the class has sadly closed.

Five Fields Away

An old man pushed through my gate - limping painfully
Up to my door
I could have sworn I'd seen him
Somewhere before.
I lifted the latch –
I'd not yet locked up -
My door was still held on the catch.
He apologised profusely
For calling so late.
"Not at all," I replied, "Though it's almost dark –
It's not much after eight."

"May I sit for a moment or two."
He enquired.
I nodded my approval – for he'd recently been in an accident
It later transpired.
He lowered himself gently onto the bench in the porch
Dislodging a flashlight –
Which (for a moment) became an untameable torch.
He sat for a while regaining his breath -
Then asked - did I know of a place where he could stay –
As he'd been born close by -
Just beyond the budding may – only five fields away.

"Five fields away – ah yes - five fields away
That must be Smalthorns Farm -
No-one lives there now." I said.
I mused silently – most of the family had come to some harm.
"That's right – that was our place."
The old man (apparently reading my thoughts) offered,
Wiping large - pale pearls of sweat from his face.
"Though I left there not long after the Second World War
When the well fell in -
Killing three men -
My father – uncle - and elder brother – yes all my male kin."

I pointed in the opposite direction saying
"Try the Rose and Crown
They have rooms
Where I'm sure you'll be able to bed down
Somewhere in there –
If you like I could give them a ring"–
But my offer was met only - with a blank stare.
Having offered - I went into the house –
Made a quick call – (I wasn't gone long)
But by my return -
The old man had already gone.

I walked into town the very next day
Where I met a woman called Nan
Whom I knew had lived at Smalthorns farm –
I asked for her help – to which she replied, "I will- if I can."
I told her of the old man –and how he had gone –
She became suddenly distressed
Saying, "That was my brother Ron."
He was killed by a car
On this very spot just a week ago yesterday -
He now lies cold – In the Old Lane Cemetery–
Just over there - only five fields away."

Floating Sidewards

Floating through the airtight door
I was drawn – unwillingly - to trip
For a timeless - surreal space journey
On an inter-galactic – health care ship.

The quiet hiss of an air valve closing
Punctuated the eternal silence of night
As the airlock sealed me in - to take
My couch - on a 'mystery testing flight'.

The hush echoed to loud trip-trappings
Of planetoids – in pale or a dark navy blue
Who appear to be cosmic incarnations
Of a (long lost) nurse care crew.

They anaesthetised with hologram smiles
And made sure we were all correctly fed -
Intravenously - through cannulas and drips -
While laid out neatly and straightened in bed.

They huddled in urgent gabbling meets
Planning to take - for all 'our own' good -
Pulses beating - pressures up – just to
Record them with our samples of blood.

Sometimes they lived in our world
Then – turned into strange cotton wool.
In our world they would simply observe us
And log down their conclusions in full.

An aging man was nil by mouth -
A heart patient thought he'd been let out -
But inner-space compilations had deemed
That - his escape was still in some doubt.

It seemed an age since we'd left
Our world of fresh air and of sun
For a deadpan place lacking a breeze
That might blow in any semblance of fun.

We rendezvoused a light year or two
Away from the planet of Mars
Where we replenished our dwindling stock
From a fleet - of re-servicing marmalade jars.

Before we journeyed for Saturn three
A suit form beamed on board.
I'm not sure where it came from -
But it materialized – just outside our ward.

"I am the doctor." it cheerily claimed,
"I'm doing a day's round of chores -
I'll ask you all some questions – but only if
I have time - will I listen to any of yours."

We were caught in a space without time
Though the clock kept going on round
I'd watched it a millennia of times
Since the day we had left our home ground.

I became ill on the day we reached a light year away
That filled the leading android with fear -
She sent for the laser general on call - who
Stated – "We only lodge healthy men here."

So the next day I was discharged - with a note
That read - 'this patient is too ill to remain.'
Now at last - with the force being with me
I've materialised on home ground once again.

Flood Repairs

Troubles come with the floods -
I 'ad t' get the Sunshine Plumber's in.
Young Kevin said, "It all be scrap".
Then Ron chucked it in the bin.
I 'adn't got much money
As the floods 'ad left me short
So I offered to pay young Kevin
With a bottle or two of Port.

And then of course
There was the Punnett Twin -
Who - when busy floorin' -
Did tile himself - completely in.
'e 'ad bedded 'em up too thick
Across the parlour floor -
About 'alf n'inch above the bottom gap
Of the tightly shut front door.

Now t' be fair 'e didn't panic -
Or that's what I've bin told -
For 'e's a man of some experience,
Bein' forty - or more years old.
'e just rose steady to 'is feet -
Before givin' out a shout
For Dave the 'andy carpenter
To come - an' let 'im out.

Dave came boundin' round
Sayin', "It's lucky I was so near
Bein' as 'ow I was 'ard at work -
Across at The Volunteer".
'e then went on to say,
"If you can't drop down the floor
I'll 'ave to get me saw out
An' cut a piece from off the door".

Once all was sorted out
Dave was persuaded by the twin
Not to let a word get out -
'cause folk might laugh at 'im.
Well all I'll say about them lads
Is - if they was bent on secrecy
Then they shouldn't 'ave let
Such gossip out – right in front of me.

Save Me - Free Me

Let me be free of wrong accusation -
The grimaces of cramp or sharp intimidation -
Nightmares – wide-awake cares -
Relieved only for a second or two
Before tension reforms anew
As a tiny mistake -
Causes sharp stomach ache -
Dyspepsia – and other unpleasant digestive affairs.

Save me from those corporate corruptions
Manifested in subliminal suggestion
Or more openly as 'call centre' selling instructions
Sent over my 'phone, voiced in by a clone
Asking, 'Do I own my own home?'
In a voice that gives me the feeling
Robert - is in fact from Darjeeling -
Put there to annoy me from a distant time zone.

Let me be free of the dog-collared speaker -
De-frocked and locked out
From all further church meetings
Forcing him to pull faces
In some very strange places
Just for a bed –
A roof over his head –
Poor food – sour drink and indifferent heating.

Save me from that chilled apprehension
That accompanies matters concerning my pension
The shiverings - the misgivings
That arrive with a warning – 'refer to the notes' -
Even if only to register my right to vote
For that government pawn -
Who sent me the form
On which I must write confirmation that I am still living.

Let me be free of death's interring grasp
His cheap, shining clasp -
Squeezing, hexagonal wood-boarded embrace -
And the six feet of earth
Threatening the remains of my worth –
The centipedes – worms and cousins of snails
Who would surely dine out on my rotting entrails
So, with appropriate grace,
Please launch my warm ashes up into space!

Frost Warning

At ten to four this morning
Winter drifted in from outside
In through my window - without warning
At ten to four this morning
The white frost on the plum – adorning
My garden - laid cover from side to side
At ten to four this morning
Winter drifted in from outside.
Once the drift had swelled
To an outright tide
I wished I had closed my window
Instead of leaving it there - open wide.
At ten to four this morning.

A Spiritual Enigma

Do ghosts see as us- from the other side?
Feel warmth within an overflowing pride-
Become – as 'bygones' – vapourise to gas-
Or - re-born with sharper senses, just as
New Year's thoughts turn toward the growing bliss
Of flora's first spring welcome, not to miss
Snowdrops courting pale lines of liquid sun -
Their shoots of winter pushing out – come
Once January days have succumbed to death –
Overcome by February's damping breath,
Breathing such a form of pre-spring greeting,
That brings fresh promise to those sweetening
Nectar drops - oozing from re-birthing spores
To make fruit from seed with flesh – bound to cores
Hatching out the growing need for calories -
In nature's '3D' orchard galleries
Or - simply take time for release of grief
Before re-birth - as psychic man's belief -
In being cosmic settlers in reverse -
Gone to a timeless - mirrored universe.

Can we confidently claim we know they
See full colour not only shades of grey?
Hear speech as we do – and un-spoken words -
Is this thought preposterously absurd?
Can they hear and at the same time be heard –
Detect the whirring of a humming bird.
Enjoy the sharp shriek of a vixen's call,
Know music from a crashing water fall,
Sense rhythm from the distant thudding beat
Of rampant buffalo's fast approaching feet.
Feel danger in a hungry viper's hiss
Enjoy his passing to the hot abyss
Slithering - no reversing rib - sliding
To bleached white carrion in hiding.
Or - simply update themselves with our lives
Acting as His observers - even spies -
Waiting there in reluctant hesitation
For man's after dark communication.-
Felt as low vibrating, fretful discord
Through stiff fingers pressed to Ouija board.

If they see and hear me then could it be -
The shadow – mute beneath the chestnut tree
Is a fleshless - boneless spirit - rather
Like that of my paternal grandfather?
He just a few years older now than me -
Frozen in earth age – that of sixty three.
Do I see him pace with stiff backed pride
And measured gait of a Gloucester's stride -
'Kitchener' stepping from his cottage door
As upright now as then – in his 'Great' War.
Breathing motionless air, no oxygen
No carbon nor traces of nitrogen -
Telepathically corresponding
Through soundless talk – in a deep responding -
Or have I seen only with my mind's eye -
Not heard the noiseless truth or silent lie?
Must I wait until I am 'body gone'
And as a poltergeist, must linger on
Or will the milling souls now deign to speak
And let slip those clear answers that I seek?

Grandma's Mixture

My Grandma's recipe contained
Sour cream and cabbage leaves
It cured malicious rumours
And deterred potential thieves.
She chopped then liquidised it
So the effect was at its best
Mixed into a bedtime drink
Or rubbed upon a poorly chest.

She added wild garlic
And shells from pullet's eggs
When rubbin' on the washin' line
And greasin' them gypsy pegs.
After dark she'd feed the hens
And pull her washin' in as well
For she could find her laundry
Just by a followin' of the smell.

She thinks her recipe's quite good
But not perfect every time
So she says, "I often put in chalk
Or just add a spoon or two of lime.
By the time the mixture cools
I find it may look a little thin
So I thicken it with badger fat
That I always stir well in."

A man once tumbled from his horse
Which he blamed my Grandma for
And says he'll never grease his saddle
With Grandma's mixture anymore.
He took her up to County Court -
But the Judge found in her favour
For he liked her mixture well enough
But frowned on his behaviour.

I haven't seen her for a while
They say she's gone away -
Some thought she was in hospital
Other's said she'd gone on holiday.
But wherever she is staying now
It will be first class no doubt -
For it was on the news the other night
That Tesco had bought her out.

An Interesting Solution

Now the compound interest calculation's done
My debts grow day by day
And I have not the wherewithall to pay.

So my credit time has all but run
And I am left to ponder as I may -
Now the compound interest calculation's done.

Perhaps my salvation lies with use of gun -
Not to end my indebted life that way
But to rob upon the Queen's highway -
Now the compound interest calculation's done.

Honey Stone

A high street set in mellow light
Now hidden by the grime
Has lost her radiant glow -
Turned dark by dirt and time.
The hiring beech was toppled
By an uncommon nightfall breeze
Gone - sawn up for firewood -
The sad end for many 'meeting trees'.

Gone too the congregation elm,
Once shade for oracle and maid -
One with finest propositions –
The other's feelings played
To court her for the hiring -
From Michaelmas - he'd pay
For half a year of skivvying,
That would not end till 'Lady Day'.

A corner washed by summer light
Is not as clean as she might show,
For a century of neglect dulls down
And stains her summer glow.
The burning sun's over light
Tones the shadows out -
Thins the cracks and chips
Of a market hall in rout.

False cut dormers punctuate
Her roof of fine grey slate
While inside - her cobbled floor
Is scored by rut and worn of pate.
Her open arches frame the views
That wait - as photographic bait -
For tourist picture snappers
Draw beneath her gabled shade till late.

The Woolstapler's hall leads back
To great men from the past
Who built up a fervent wool trade
That simply could not last.
But the structures that they left –
Both ramshackle and sublime -
Stand as wool men's legacy
To a town - built to last as long as time.

At Rest on Hill 60

My burning face turns chill
Once on the windward side of bitter hill
Where unseen sheets of pliant rage
Wheeze in - to turn the page
On winter's berthed distress -
Upstaging her unpleasantness -
Already whipped into my face -
Swirling at a thunderous pace
With winter's kiss biting deep -
Long into my restless sleep
Where I dream and make
A wish - that I might wake
Far from this night address
Of winter and her harsh caress -
That I sense comes as the kiss of death
For I smell its scent upon her breath.

His marching place was chill
Exposed upon that killing hill
Where useless carnage stifled rage -
Carnage unheralded on a page
Recording morbid lists of distress
Without pity or unpleasantness -
Seen etched upon the staring face
Of each man still holding pace
With the sore morass – so deep
It takes away the chance to sleep
And dream and make
The flowers bloom again before they wake
From that callous field address
Caught in rigours harsh caress -
That they sense comes as the kiss of death
For they smell its scent upon her breath.

House Call

The wood nymph stood in earnest
At the elf's front door,
On the winding shingle path
Where she once stood before.
She was about to lift his latch,
When she saw clearly glued
To his door - a poorly written note
With words extremely rude.

She had hoped the elf would help
As she must face the cost
Of just one shilling spent
And a further sixpence lost.
The note said all those tall enough
Would get nothing out of him
And those too short to read the note
Must assume he wasn't in.

It went on to say – "to save
Would be so very wise
For those who come for money
Will receive a blank surprise.
But those who thought they wouldn't
Would be much better off
For they wouldn't waste their time
Straining - at the empty trough".

She turned and caught her toe
On something navy blue
Which caused her bells to ring -
What was she supposed to do?
She picked the object up,
Took the frayed elastic out
And mended her old catapult -
Then shot a jumping trout.

"Mr Trout," said she, "It is your fault
For you know that you should aughter
Stay within your rainbow shoal
Safely swimming in the water".
The river was your home
But now it will be that monger bloke
Not that this is personal Trout,
It's just that I am broke."

The monger gave her fourp'nce
For her errant fish
Saying that the elf had ordered one
As it was his favourite dish.
He said he couldn't pay her more
For such a skimpy thing
But he would give her sixp'nce
Just to hear her toe bells ring.

She had to dance a hornpipe,
Highland jig and salty reel
Which caused her bells to ring -
But shook off her left shoe heel.
She tripped out to the cobbler
Who said "I'll mend your shoe no doubt
But I won't take your money
For I want paying with a trout."

So she waited for the miser elf,
Limping homeward with the gout
And helped him to his drab front door
Where - he somehow lost his trout.
Which luckily she found
As she went dancing on her way
To the cobblers for her shoe
Now she had the wherewithal to pay.

The cobbler then returned to her
The shoe as good as new,
While the fishman was content
With the ringing nymphet's shoe.
The elf- of course - was cursing
As he ate his frog spawn stew
And the wood nymph smiled as she recalled
That cast off garb of navy blue.

In Absentia

As no man more innocent stood in England's docks
To face such cruel aspersions cast in a bristling glee
So he should be freed from pillory - in the village stocks

Those who swear an oath in the witness box
Should not speak false in hope to banish he
As no man more innocent stood in England's docks

The man accused would help to heal or cure a pox
But would not harm a garden slug nor hurt a flea
So he should be freed from pillory - in the village stocks

All you fair maids in your bonnets and your frocks
Should not be out to scorn but back at home for tea
As no man more innocent stood in England's docks

Such a man so troubled beneath his greying locks
Was not there to hear or even have an eye to see
So he should be freed from pillory - in the village stocks

We should all be distant from the man who mocks
And tell those harsh in judgement to set the poet free
As no man more innocent stood in England's docks
So he should be freed from pillory - in the village stocks.

Instructive Reading

Reading evidence given - pre interceding
So I can avoid being fooled
By the accused's scurrilous try at fielding
My impeccable judgement
With a poor ploy of over-tearfully pleading.

Reading the amount they'd be needing
Of blood on the drip
Before exposing the gash that is readily bleeding,
Following the crash
That was caused by over-exuberant speeding.

Reading gardening advice before yielding
To the task of raking
And composting the results of my weeding
Then mulching the bed well
Before I embark on my early spring seeding.

Reading reports on those supposedly heeding
Dietary advice to ensure
That none of them here are caught in impeding
Their way back to health
By fatuous excuses to justify their 'over' feeding.

Reading in-between lines prior to proceeding
With a marital union -
To further be satisfied the signs aren't misleading
And I'm not being trapped into conceding
My natural good sense over choice
When it comes to the start of a programme for breeding.

Up the Az'on Road

I stopped to talk to Jim
Somewhere up the Az'on Road
Which 'e said 'ad confused 'im some -
Cos 'e thought the road was closed.
But 'e did calm down a lot
When 'e 'eard what I proposed –
A broadcast to make 'im famous –
Which 'e might enjoy - 'e then supposed.

For I 'ad recently bin contacted
by a (sort of a fancy) talkin' bloke -
Who said as 'ow 'e was with the BBC
Which must a bin true - by the proper way 'e spoke.
I 'ad met 'im in the street - sat on the elm tree seat -
'e shouted out – to be 'eard above the traffic din -
That, 'e'd rung me three times last week
Before 'e 'ad bin told - I'd never 'ad the 'phone put in."

'e'd 'eard tell as I was the mon
Who 'e was obliged t' see –
For t' give ''im ''elp in makin'
'is rustic documentary - for the BBC.
For if there are any old characters left -
'e'd bin assured I'd know where they'd be found
As I'd lived 'ere all me life
An' accordin'ly must know me way around.

I explained this all t' Jim
An' got such a positive reply -
When 'e said 'e'd talk about Perce Hartley's pigs
An' the (special) nettles round their sty.
Jim claimed they was carefully planted–
A variety 'e didn't know, which soon grew very 'igh -
An' 'e knew the lad who 'ad grown em -
An' - what's more - 'e knew the reason why.

Jim said, "I quite likes that young mon -
Though there's some as thinks ''im bad.
But I knowed 'is mother - long afore 'e was born
An' the lad's only complaint is - 'e's never known 'is dad.
I know 'e 'as a reputation but 'e's not done 'alf
What they says 'e 'as - which I finds t' be quite sad -
Besides which - 'e supplies' me with 'is 'ome grown 'bacca
Which is – (by far) - the best I've ever 'ad.

I though 'is knowledge of cider apples
Would make a better piece –
Or even 'is years of pickin' sprouts
Or the time ''e took up keeping geese.
"Ah," says Jim, "We'll give that BBC mon some cider
An' a plate of sprouts and boiled beef
Then – once we 'ave 'im mellered -
We'll get 'im on - this (special) bacca leaf."

Jim could not be discouraged -
Or persuaded - to deviate from his culinary bate -
Which caused me some anxiety
For the lastin' fate - of me (new come) 'broadcastin' mate' –
But the time an' date were set
For our plates of sumptuous grub
It was to be eaten just before
Our broadcast - at the Eight Bells (country pub).

A good crowd 'ad gathered there
In the 'kitchen' of the Bells -
Drawn in by all the excitement
And some rich an' weird smells.
Once the toasts were said
We inhaled Woodbine smoke which came as some relief
When coupled to the aroma of pipes of that rough cut shag -
Then despair – when I clearly smelt the waft of that (special) bacca leaf.

By the time the programme started
Goin' out - across the airwaves live -
It was nearly six-o-clock
Though we should ''ave begun at 'alf past five.
By now that BBC bloke was full - of (special) bacca smoke
Which I didn't think was fair
An' encouraged by ol' Jim – swore while live on air - told a dirty joke or two -
Then fell from off 'is chair.

A riot shortly follered an' the police were then called -
As the clamour turned to uproar -
When the swellin' crowd that 'ad gathered
Chanted – 'that they wanted more.'
Those radio folk were quick –with their equipment - to withdraw
Leavin' their director crying, "Oh it's all such an awful mess!"
But we locals stayed an' cheered ol' Jim
For 'is arrangement of - such a smoke invoked success.

Cherry Minding

Campden 'ad many orchards years agoo -
On the Leasows was an odd 'un.
Then across the Aston High Road -
All the way over t' Whaddon.
The trees was aluz 'ealthy -
Well watered and well fed -
Guarded by the cherry-minder
'rose up early - from 'is 'orse 'air bed.

Ol' Percy Pitcher
Was one such early riser -
For 'e lived all on 'is own
An' was thought to be a miser.
'e'd get on 'is ol' bike
An' cycle from 'is 'ome
With two quarts o' cider,
A loaf an' a ol' pork bone.

Ol' Perce 'ad no wireless
For t' give 'im a merry tune -
So 'e played 'is music
With 'is tin plate an' wooden spoon.
But this was drowned completely
By 'im a 'ittin' a rusty oil drum lid -
With a large lead sash weight -
Which is what ol' Percy did.

'is job was quite well done
But it wasn't much well paid.
Just enough for t' buy some grub -
An' cider - often roughly made.
As the fruit becum more ripe
He'd 'ave to goo an' pick -
Along with all them women -
Which made a fyow among 'em sick.

They 'ad purple Pershore's
An' egg plums put in chips,
Set down in the cool part
Of them ridge an' furrer dips.
An' then there was Victoria's,
In the pockets of 'er frock
An' the ones that she called win'falls -
'idden, in the 'em-line of 'er smock.

Well they all went on to damsons
A'ter they 'ad finished with the plums,
Which was then follered by the apples,
An' ater that - whatever comes.
By now the mornin's wasn't bright
An' offen covered with a mist,
Which caused ol' Percy's mis'ap
When 'is bike lurched into a ditch.

By the time they women found 'im
'is red face 'ad turned to blue.
An' 'is cider bottle, it 'ad broke
So they knew not what to do.
For up till then they 'ad relied
On ol' Percy's cider as the spray,
They used t' sooth the midge bites
An' keep all them flies away.

Well now many years 'ave passed
An' Percy's bike 'as turned to rust -
'Is body's passed from bein' ashes
An' gone an' turned to dust.
But many women still remembers
Back to that fateful day,
When they 'ad to change their way
Of keepin' all them flies at bay.

Joining the Dark Side

I'd come to join the dark side
Putting all good thoughts at bay -
Created a gothic home
And let the black mistress in to stay.
Then I'd organize a right surprise
Invite the devil and his wife to play -
Then advertise those cheats and lies
Far beyond a million miles away.

I'd have black clad - lady Goths
Fluttering around like rubber moths –
Butterflies of the night
Restricted (by their chains) from taking flight.
Held to two dimensional dancing –
Nervously glancing
Into each other's faces -
Images of (dead pan) blank spaces.

All would be mine – to do with as I like –
My black satin - sheeted bed -
Playing host to the ghost of deviant intercourse -
Stained red by sexual dread –
Magic - choked by studded collar
Unclean
Soiled by a weird –
Dark – satanic joy machine.

A secret ward
Where the Marquis de Sade
Becomes the bard
His teachings put onto hard plastic card.
By his disciples –
Bejewelled in icicles
Those Marys and Michaels
Wed over their motorized cycles.

Their music played on creaking leather
And the clanking of - the heavily chained -
Enslaved to Satan's pleasure -
By whom they're caught and trained.
Manacled –
Weighted down - chrome barnacled -
Their cries and screams
Luring me - ever deeper into their demonic dreams.

Last Words

There I saw him stood,
Grey and bent and worn,
His wild eyes just staring points
Abandoned and forlorn.
The words he had to say
Were hard for him to speak,
Between each gasping breath
And pulse now beating weak.

I beckoned him to sit,
Offering to him my arm
But he preferred to stand
Expecting no more harm.
His height, reduced and stooped
Was less than I remember,
He had the ashen countenance
Of a man in deep December.

His hand stretched, trembling,
Blue black ink filled veins
Marking sallow skin with lines
Like those on past remains.
Unstraightening, callused fingers
Stretched to make their point,
Gnarled by painful fleshy nodes
Swelling each arthritic joint.

His ageing – greying - welling,
Red rimmed, tear filled eyes
Spoke - before the words
Of his final sad surprise.
For the taking of his stock
Followed by his dying wife,
Were replaced, he smiled, by tumours
Which were there to end his life.

He gave to me his watch,
A pen-knife from his coat
And a roughly folded parchment
Upon which was there fresh wrote,
"My sins are balance weighed
All my earthly debts are paid.
So now I leave - without shame
And nought but my good name."

At this his failing legs
Gave him cause to rest.
He dropped upon a fallen log -
His hands clasped to his chest.
His final words went unheard
As they blew among the trees.
I had no chance to hear them -
Gone – like spinning sycamore keys.

I stooped to call on his remains
But his last breath had gone.
Gone to find his resting wife
And join with her as one.
I vowed an oath out load,
As I stood there quite alone,
I would have his words recorded
And carved upon his stone.

Leaving for Duty

Rain clouds dull the breaking dawn
Low – black – thick
Across the heaving decks
Lined with young men being sick.
Each one uniformed – anonymous
Deck hand, green stick sailors -
Volunteer prisoners of His Majesty -
Kept keen by Naval 'Gaolers'.

All now heave and retch as one –
A teenaged apprentice boiler maker -
Weekend crooner - his piano tuner -
Stammering assistant undertaker
Freckled sprinter - typeset printer -
Gaunt young men – (though trembling) – steadfast
Praying that they will not quake
When duty calls them to the mast.

Bilious green - tonsil disgorged seas
Beat about their listing home
As if intent on turning a creaking bark
Into a greasy - deep sea metal tomb -
Dragged down to rake the scrabbid floor
And lie broke beneath the waves -
To be whispered of in future -
As (one of many) ocean graves.

Though the ocean herself may not smash
These fine (legal) buccaneers
To the bottom of their mindings -
Knotted in the belly of their rightful fears -
But – instead – leave them
To those undercurrent metal shark's
Dispatch of stinging fish -
Sent hot - with a rush of lethal sparks.

Or - fate may prevent a scattering
Of debris blown from bow to stern
With the turning of the spitting fish - to miss -
So their searing sparks don't burn
And this convoy guard survives
The waiting watery grave – un-surpassed -
Her survival through ice and pain
Not first - nor (hopefully) will it be the last.

Left in the Dark

As the afternoon and evening merge
Into approaching dusk
So we are left blown around
Or, as in mud stuck to the ground
Like winnowed empty husk.

Our thoughts dashed and then delivered
To an unmanned host
From heads not too bright
Unheard and out of sight
Save by the prowling ghost.

Our appetite for consuming thought
Now is slowed to crawl
With the cooling of our will
By this unpleasant evening chill
That suffuses from within each weeping wall.

Our eyes can no longer make out the shape
That will even more mature
Through the shadow's murk
In which those forming dangers lurk
To slink, as starving wolf amid our own discomfiture.

The darkness and the storm conspire
To billow out and blow about
The wet of dripping missal -
Till grown to gale's high pitched whistle
Blowing a double reeded tune to maximize our doubt.

The storm's crescendo smothers laughing light
And cuts the man-made power back.
With no pricking glow of stars to peak
Nor mirror moon's spotlight beams to leak
The sky corsairs attack – out from the threatening black.

Amid the tempests dire destruction
Strode the bile and smoke striped cat
Having seen everything with all
She lets vent her distressing well-known caterwaul
For the bitter queen is forced to wait upon the outside mat.

Loneliness

Loneliness closed the gate
On laughter's path up to the moon.
A creamy silken crescent
(Carelessly hung)
Angled in a charcoal sky -
Casting light and (therefore) shadows
Of the travellers passing by -
Below the moon -
Trapped like sticky crumbs adhered to a china plate
Or ashes - spent in the cooling grate.

Loneliness pitches the wearer
Head over knees and heels -
Like a child's iron hoop -
Or turning wheels rounding the loop –
On an unmetalled road
(Shaking the bones)
Of the hapless traveller
Pleading to become an erstwhile reveller -
Dancing amid the kinder – fairer -
Smiling – amorphous - wayfarers.

Loneliness is held behind the wire -
Strung across the path out to the lea
Where passions dance
Among the daisy throws -
In shear silken hose -
(Tastefully held)
By satin garters of merriment
Worn – beyond banal experiment -
But still far from the scented ash log fire -
Beyond rusted barbs strung out across the mire.

Summer solstice madrigal circles form - around
The growing shoots of loneliness -
Stretching high toward the sky
In youthful - callow - willow fashion -
Seeking out compassion
From amidst June's blue haze
And floating virginal shrouds
Of pale - cotton boll clouds –
But high altitude's cold surround
Sends green shoots hurtling back again -
Still seeking emotional – (unfound) common ground.

Looking East

The distant pallid yellow light
Reached - as though on ration -
To as much as touch our dark surrounds
In timid - almost ghostly fashion
And light the empty hedgerow twigs
Bare - unmoving – silent – black -
Sparsely dappled, in a cold - silver
Skim - across the blackthorn's back.

This dull reflecting footlight fades
As poor candle power's yield
Dims through the midnight hour
To lose the frozen crystal field -
Quiet – motionless – now hidden
Backdrop to the deadly play
Of we – un-bespoke dealers
Of game on which – we darkly prey.

Unseeing eyes of we unseen spies
Strain towards the east
For a sign of red morning glow
To light up our desparate feast.
So we are cast by blanket cloud
Onto an alien stage of blindness -
Stood as dormant shivering wretches -
Wrapped with neither overcoat nor kindness.

Shackled by promise – we cannot leave
But stay - to make good our vow
Of a fully laden - for-dawn return
And put food on the plate somehow.
We hope (under promise) to catch
A leaping hare - ground rabbit or two
And by avoiding shark-toothed gins -
Deliver such morsels - long overdue.

Lost September

Warm September – still –
As I remember -
Ushered in by hedgling smoke
And greying folk
Caught - in their November –
Humping sheaves and clearing leaves
Ready for the winnowing and turning -
Or the fire - set for burning.

Soft September – calm –
As I remember –
Worked by helpful neighbour
Volunteering labour
To shovel corn and ember –
For bread and to be spread –
Ready to bear sacks of grain at will
If only he could find a working flour mill.

Broad September – yearned –
As I remember –
For those salad lunches
Of radish and spring onion bunches -
Tomato, lettuce and outdoor - mature cucumber -
For her thanksgiving barns
Filled with harvest riches -
Flowing free like fresh edged ditches.

Late September – flat –
As I remember –
Left far behind
In fair light (of a kind)
Shed by October's even temper –
And the gaze of fair weather days -
Right for drying late corn -
Potatoes, barley and maize -
Sifted through the shade of autumn haze.

Cool September – gone
Into a cold November -
A dark November of short reason -
Treason - plot and spitting ember -
That's where September fell -
As I remember.

Madame Cézanne

Wife
of the
famous French
painter.
From a portrait
of her painted
by him.

Brushed by age and grime
Washed out by seas of time -
Battered by their ebb and flow -
Weathered as though battered
By sleet and crystal snow.
Yet warm – not vulgar or course -
Nor found gripped by remorse.

Enigmatic – thoughtful -
Greying - though not dull.
Musing – though not confused –
Harsh treated though not misused.
Stressed though not distressed
Caught made up – full dressed.

Never labelled as loose
Nor considered obtuse –
In dark - tightly done coat -
Simply seeming remote
Under practical hair
Cut (modest in style)
But – it seems - tended with care.

None the less
Still fresh – as though blessed –
Beyond the brush strokes
Her image provokes
Presentation (beyond breath)
Well struck – beyond death.

McGregor

I remember McGregor
A very smelly beggar -
From somewhere up north -
A man of small worth
Who came around every spring
With a bell that he'd ring -
Asking for old rabbit skins
And any copper scrap things.

He went off with our Auntie's cat
Grandma's best hat –
A boiled ham left on the cill
Put out there to chill –
As well as our neighbour's wife
The light of his life –
Yes I remember McGregor
A very smelly beggar.

Miss Emma Dundee

I was sitting at home
Playing with paper and comb
The tune – Waltzing Matilda
To a Punnett twin builder
When I was invaded by a tropical bee
I was soon to discover –
Was Miss Emma Dundee.

She came in pulling a trolley
Which she denied had fallen
From the back of a lorry -
As she said, "You have something
Of which I am fond –
So I must have
Your maturing - Prudential Bond."

I said, "This bond is mine
I've had it quite some time
So please leave my home
And find a bond of your own."
To which she replied,
"I've just come from Australia
Where I was never a failure."

She added, "My brother travels miles
Just to wrestle crocodiles –
He's known as Champion Jim
And I'm better than him."
So I handed over my bond
With a rather grim smile
And (hopefully) - a modicum of style.

She then thanked me -
Saying, "She could see
That I lived very well -
It was obvious
From such a wonderful smell."
So I quickly relented
And handed over
My breakfast - as well.

Meadow and Moor

Cold night pours scorn over light
Scolding me
With her crusty guffaw
Drawing me down – deeper - into the night
As she whispers – coarsely,
"Pile up your utilities neatly in sets
Stack them into (playing hard) packs
And then shuffle - all those unpaid regrets."

The midnight mountain loomed -
A barrier
That must be traversed
Or I am surely doomed - marooned
In cold night's words -
Expressed with chilling delight -
Like an unfaithful wife
Caught up in marital spite.

"Play for the gallery - play for the crowd."
The cold night cries -
From somewhere out in the harshest of skies -
"Play hard – play long and loud –
But hear the creaking
Of rigor and more –
Hear the raw winds howl at your door."

She has the horizon – the meadow and moor
While I am betwixt
And between – in a fix
That is chafing me raw.
Can I make haste to the bright light of day?
Away from her
And her cuffing guffaw
Over the horizon - to meadow and moor.

"Chase all you like – or choose to withdraw
From the fight
For I will scatter your lights."
Cries her Harshness, the Darkess of Night.
"Your cards are all played
And your regrets - all still are unpaid."
Scuffs her scruffy guffaw -
Over the horizon – to meadow and moor.

My Uncle Jack

My uncle Jack was in the army
Through the years between the wars -
Then 'e went out chimney sweepin' -
But 'e doesn't anymore.
Not since 'is embarrassment –
(Or so I've 'eard it said)–
When 'e shoved 'is rods so 'ard
'e pushed a woman out o' bed.

'e was a sweepin' at an 'ouse
Near the Lygon Arms
When 'e cured the Lady's ailments
With ''is expert roddin' charms.
She said, "I believe I had the vapours,
As reported - in the highbrow papers.
Though I'm still not sure just what has cured me – but -
I believe it was a shot - of intravenous soot."

'e swept Mrs Keeley's chimney once
In a cottage by the church
An' was (unfairly) blamed
For leavin' 'er in the lurch –
When a nasty rumour
Went buzzin' round the town
That it was 'is savage sweepin'
That 'ad brought 'er cottage down.

There was a woman in the Lion
Who swore Jack's sweepin' was the best
An' advised all those doubters
To put 'im to the test.
Her friend said "I know it's true –
'cause my neighbour - Mrs Bailey
Admires Jack's roddin' skills so much -
That she has 'im round twice daily."

Then Jack took on the task
Of clearin' moles from off the squire's lawn –
A job that should be done
(accordin' to ol' Bronc) well afore the dawn –
An' the stuff t' use be gun powder -
Or - if tryin' not to disturb the peace
Then spread a layer on liberally -
Of maturin' mutton grease.

Now Jack got down to spreadin grease
But by 'alf way 'e'd run out and needed more.
So 'e spread on a tub of army issue Brylcream
'e 'ad liberated from Lahore.
Now the lady of the 'ouse went puce
And threatened they would sue –
Cos the squire couldn't speak
As 'e was quietly a chokin'- while turnin' navy blue.

So Jack left the manor – (through the kitchen door)
With a plate of fairy cakes – a fresh baked loaf of bread
An' a brace o' well 'ung pheasants -
That 'e liberated – from in the pottin' shed.
Then 'e peddled to the 'Lion' – (feelin' very pleased)
As 'e felt 'e'd drove them moles way -
So - all in all - 'e would 'ave to say
'e 'ad indeed 'ad - a very edifyin' day.

Misnomers

Names thought up in a hurry
Cause their holders vexation and worry
Trying to cope with a name that just doesn't fit -
About as much use as the flame on a candle
That's yet to be lit -
Or a joke told without a vestige of wit.

Names too quickly arranged
For Christenings, that later are changed
In an attempt to repair damage already done
By being called after a matinee idol -
Or tearaway son gone on the run -
Into a life without even one day of fun.

Names affecting a career in sport
As when following a rough tackle – well caught
By an over zealous referee late on in the game
Who yells, "One man's already sent off
And you'd go the same
Way - if I could only remember your name."

Names needed to be mentioned
When filling out claims for state pensions
On forms that must be sent in by due cut-off date,
Filled out correctly to avoid loss of benefit,
Or the late
Issue - of a fuel allowance rebate.

Names sewn into school shorts -
Indelibly printed in travellers passports,
Or given to girls for the years they're a miss
Only to be lost by the exchanging of the rings
And then wedding kiss
That starts a future of uncertain bliss.

Names needed to record a new birth,
To print on all papers assessing one's worth,
Written in triplicate to follow us during the rise
And then fall of our dull ordinary lives,
So the need for a full name is of little surprise
At the recording of each man's sad demise.

Nan's Niggles

I met Nan outside St. Catharine's door,
You should 'ave 'erd 'er cuss,
For she'd just missed the outing bus,
A thing she'd never done before.

I said, "Nan! never you fear
By the time you'd 'ave got there
The beach would a bin covered in chairs
So you'm better off stayin' right 'ere."

"Ah," says she, "being late's what I tries t' avoid
'cause missing a day in the sun
By the sea - isn't much fun -
It makes me feel so very annoyed.

And I 'aven't had much luck of late -
Last Wednesday I missed the club
Where they 'ad fish 'n chips for grub -
'cause I went and wrote down the wrong date."

Then she said, "A fox came t'uther night,
Which was extremely unpleasant -
As 'e chased after me Indian pheasant
And that give me a 'ell of a fright.

So now I've blocked off his track
With a roll of barbed wire
And an old lorry tyre
But you can bet that 'e'll try and come back."

She said that last week they'd all been to Weston
But the wind 'ad chapped her lips
As well as blowin' sand on her chips -
Which played 'avoc with her indigestion.

Then they 'ad to dash 'elter-skelter -
When hail battered the pier
Causing the whole group to fear
They might be stuck without further shelter.

She continued to say that while on the beach
She'd gone in the sea for a dip -
Which caused the lifeguards to flip
When they thought she had strayed out of reach.

Two lads in black trunks and white vest
Ran into the sea with a shout -
Before roughly escorting her out
Saying, 'she was lucky she was not under arrest.'

Next to Her

Her animated fringe
Of shining chestnut hair
Suggested to the boy in me
That she had charm to spare.

Her high boned cheeks
Were coloured to a nervous flush -
Could it be me who'd caused
Such a perfect face to blush?

The fluttering of her lashes
Told me I should beware
But I was so drawn to her
That I really didn't care.

Her soft plum lips then parted
To let the faintest smile out
With such a strong allure
They had no need to pout.

Her scant frame was dressed
With gentle curves so spare
I felt she would be damaged
If a crude advance caught her unaware.

But from my fading dream
I knew nothing would occur
When I saw she held the manly hand
Of the woman sitting next to her.

No Breakfast

I woke to breakfast -
A nightmare from out of my dream -
There was not a scraping of butter –
Only that easy to spread margarine,
To put on to toast that was burnt to a cinder -
Instead of beige or light brown
Or a shade that's somewhere between -
It was at least three dark shades below
A disgruntled black crow
Before he's had time for his morning preen.

A cup of cold coffee
Was knocked over by me -
Just another mistake - as I had wanted tea -
With a drop of skimmed milk
By now resembling thick cream
Slightly rancid - but labelled fat free -
Which I threw out with the toast
Soon devoured by that gluttonous crow
Whom I feel - is far luckier than me.

The corn flakes are stale -
That I bought cheap in a sale
And the mould on the crumpet's a blow
To my wilting chance
Of consuming the requisite fuel
To help me trudge out through the snow -
For a hard day at work
From which I'm tempted to shirk
Because the way that I feel –
I just might not bother to go.

No Horses Now

No horses now -
Only tractors pull the plough -
The drill – till the loam
And draw the harvest home.
No milkmaid now
Only automated - lactated cow -
No apple crunching sow
Beneath the orchards (shedding) bough.
No stooks of corn
Or cherry minder's raucous dawn
Only hybrid corn and trees -
Too low to brush the breeze.
No orchard sandwich basket
Or cider demijohn - bound in wicker casket.
Simply tractor driven boom
Flaying noble fruits to their (pulpated) doom.

No buckets of swill -
Over filled and spilled
Across the (padded) hard -
Chicken cleansed yard -
No raised high ricks
On staddle stone sticks
Only giant straw bales
Built back to back
In urban sized stacks
Behind post and wire rails -

No iron tyres on chipped stone drive
Nor willing hands at work by five -
Just satellite controlled machines
Rolling over alien rustic scenes -
No raucous goose
Nor wooden barrels of apple juice -
Only orange string
And blue polythene bags - blowing loose
Across the yard where
We do not see - horses now -
Replaced by tractor pulling plough
Drilling – tilling loam -
Straining - snorting not –
To draw the harvest home.

Under Blessed

Ol' Bert was laid out to rest
In 'is old trilby 'at –
An' a gold an' navy cravat -
Worn to enhance 'is Sunday best.
"It was pin striped y' know –
Brown double breasted – an' much under tested."
It was then suggested -
By 'is agin' - sister-in-law, Mo.

Bert's widow Lil
Said. "Explain clearly Maureen –
Just what it is that you mean –
'cos your remarks are making me ill."
"Oh! I meant nothing – my dear
I quite liked dear ol' Bert
The irrepressible flirt."
Whispered Mo - in her sister's (well bejewelled) ear.

"Enough." The 'rinsed blue' widow cried -
"It has always been a great source of pride
That Bert and I never (at least to each other) lied
And I was happy to be Bert's - fourth - or fifth bride.
Mo then blurted "But Bert was so under-blessed."
To which Lil replied, "Not all the time though -
I'll have you know Mo –
It was apparent only - when he was undressed."

Lil then thought for a while
About all that her sister had said -
Especially Bert's problems in bed
And of Mo's fluttering - over rouged smile.
And then finally retorted,
"You jealous bitch
No matter how hard you wished
It was me that 'e called on and courted."

"It might be true what you've said -
But 'e was always breaking new ground
On 'is baker's round."
Moaned Mo, " 'is faults came only in bed.
After all there was that Gladys Small –
An' then Charlotte Grey -
As well as 'er young sister May
With these young girls 'e 'ad no real luck at all."

Poor ol' Bert died sat by the fire -
Pushin' a bent piece of old wire
Into the stem of 'is favourite briar -
Though I feel that it should be said -
Ol' Bert was always a trier –
'specially with 'is weakness laid bare
In a way thee an' me
Would not 'ave it be -
'cos us men feels women's words - be often sorely unfair.

November Fall

November sheds her litter bracts
Leaving trees balding sapless, dry and crusty -
Ageing wrinkled copper, cream and rusty -
Strewn across the rutted track
In blustery drifts they flow –
As a kaleidoscope - of psychedelic snow.

Trees gaunt - gnarled – livery tossed -
Become lost – ground to compost -
Mounds of black and blacker dross
Chewed by muted worms
To be broken down by December's frost.

Trunks of bone and oak share a fate -
Once both great - one spoken of as late –
Out of date - crushed to under soil bait.

Off-White Flotsam

An off-white cloud of flotsam
Dithered from the passing storm
Dry of capacity to let more
She swirls without shape or form.
Becalmed against a calmer sky
Sapped now of all her steady rain
De-humidified to vanish
Un-moist - unseen - unfelt again.

Boxing Hares

There - sitting spread on nature's grassy chairs
I was drawn to see a rabbit - from a coppice hop -
To watch a pair of early March's boxing hares.

Meanwhile a titled Lady's jewelled affairs
Left by magpie's beak while she was seen to drop
There - sitting spread on nature's grassy chairs.

For she was so quickly taken unawares
Having left her window blowing at the top
To watch a pair of early March's boxing hares.

No law and order person came to hear her cares
For they were out in search of litter louts to cop
There - sitting spread on nature's grassy chairs.

Where they were kicked by two young mares
Surprised to come upon a rabbit sat full crop
To watch a pair of early March's boxing hares.

So the lady cried upon the sloping grassy stairs
For her jewels are took and a rabbit has her stop
There - sitting spread on nature's grassy chairs
To watch a pair of early March's boxing hares.

At the Grave Side

He was one of the best – salt of the earth
I'm really going to miss my old mate Jim.
But it's not that long ago you said "Jim was no good".
When was that!
Just after lunch – on the day that you felt cause t'sack him.

I'm not having that – you take those words back
I'd never say such a thing – not on your life.
Well I'll not take it back 'cause it's true.
Come on then why would I say such a thing?
Because you were convinced he was after your dear wife.

Look! my sorrow's quite genuine – I knew him for years -
He never told lies - nor went behind any man's back.
He didn't need to with you always taking his part.
Ok, then tell me of just once when I defended old Jim.
Well! For one - there was that time when I gave him the sack.

You were incapable of treating us right.
Oh! And what makes you say that.
Remember the time Jim rescued your lad from under that dray?
Of course, but he recovered so how could that have upset old Jim.
Because it made him late for work and you docked some money from his pay.

All that was years ago and old Jim never bore me any malice
So let's shake hands and put an end to this bickering and strife
I'm happy to do that – after all it was such a long time ago.
That's the spirit – from now on we'll be the best of friends.
Well not as friendly I hope - as Old Jim was - with your second wife.

The Crown of Overbeck

Under the well greened
Dry stone walling,
I found her -
Gnarled - some amputee limbs –
Others full -
Leaning - lying,
Propped from falling.

Topping the scarp
Sat such glee -
Arching over
Green shoots of hope
On shear slope,
Dramatically plunging –
Down to the sea.

Above me she spread,
As though pleading
For her fragile brood
Of pink, blooming
Magnolia 'Flamingos' - wings spread -
Hearts spilling maroon
As if bleeding.

She was pointing above
And down to the south -
Commanding me
To look out
Over the palms -
Out to Salcombe's
White slavering mouth.

I hope to stand again
Below the green lawned deck
To gaze skyward
Through her fledging jewels -
Perched pink,
On the tilting crown
Of Overbeck.

Pierre Magnol 17th C botanist named the magnolia tree species

Paper Clippings

Old newspaper pages now newly discovered
Over drawer bottoms where for years they have covered
Dried black and red stains – carved initials with stories to tell,
Franked George VI stamps - old coins as well.
A variety of dates appear from out of the past,
Over my life - still with those shadows they cast
Over events and of people now gone
Reinforcing my need to turn pages on.

Live stock markets, weather and farming reports
Names of those caught and their fines from magistrates' courts.
Photos of sports teams, some standing some kneeling
With facial expressions that lack discernible feeling.
School governors with glares that generate dread
Sitting - posing at an oak table around the school Head
As the carnival Queen smiles with her young page boy brother
Now a granddad - as she is now, thrice a grandmother.

Yellowed and creased, short crust pages play host
To brittle and tarnished long forgotten dark ghosts -
Their (close up) pictured poses become part of obituary,
Written as a maudlin account of a life long gone into history,
Between (improving memory) pills someone is hoping to sell
And gentlemen's long-legged underwear displayed there as well.
A Middlesex batsman groomed with a famous hair cream
And an electronic flat iron that can produce jets of steam.

I read with a good deal of inquisitive zeal
About a life I remember but can no longer feel,
From newspaper articles of times that seemed jaded,
Written on sepia paper with ink that has faded.
Some teachers' obituaries are read, then discarded
About people now gone, who thought me retarded.
Gone perhaps to a place of rest in heavens knows where.
If so - they may view me differently, if we should meet again there?

Passions Unfulfilled

Passions spilled – but not fulfilled,
Was her haunting epithet,
One she was in earnest to forget.

But fate – it seemed had willed
She would be vacant – left 'to let'.
Passions spilled – but not fulfilled.

Cool beats her heart, emotions chilled
For want of warming eyes - as yet unmet.
Trapped in homeliness - to fret
Passions spilled – but not fulfilled.

Life's Passing Tides

Until the passing tides of life run dry
We must catch all the answers that we can
And adapt those inspirations flowing by.

We must throw out the lurking jealous spy
And guard against his demolition plan -
Until the passing tides of life run dry.

We must in all earnest keenly try
To keep our rantings down - and ban
All doubts which take the mind of any man -
Until the passing tides of life run dry.

Precocious

Aged the youngest - just a day past three
She was brought into the drawing room
And there- sat upon a metaphoric knee.

Where a new career was planned
Requiring her legs to swing
While she blossomed - atop a famous grand.

The pianist sat to play the opened keys
While she swung to entertain
From her tiny toes up to her dimpled knees.

She tossed her hair of strawberry blond
To hold the watching throng
Sat - (as though enchanted) by her waving curly wand.

She was then put out to entertain
For needed family wealth
And such needs must precede any search for fame.

But a life once filled with childhood pains
Has a mother's body now
But somewhere hidden- deep within - the little girl remains.

Well! Red

I fancied a blond girl
So shyly divine
But for all my wooing
She - fancied only my wine.
Maybe it was her knees
That caused me to make passes
But her hostile riposte
Was, "I think you need glasses."

Though crestfallen
I would not be bested
I disdainfully replied
"I've recently had my eyes tested."
The optician commented –
"Your eyes are just fine –
Just don't try using them
Both - at the same time".

"No! not spectacles."
She interjected -
"Your eye test came out
Just as I would have expected -
I'm talking of cut crystal
Bell mouthed or fluted."
"I'll see what I have."
In falsetto - I hooted.

"Just give me a bottle"
She tetchily insisted -
I read the label -
Though my eyes were slightly misted –
"It's a Californian appellation -
Looks like Alcatraz."
I said - as she took the bottle
Remonstrating, "It's clearly Shiraz."

Just give me a good claret
Or better still a Girgondas
And you'll see that I can be -
A most appreciative lass.
So make sure I'm well kept
In a good vintage red wine
And I'm sure you will find
That we get on just fine."

Rime Frost

Rime frost cloaks the stubble field
With a white lace smock
Under cover of the trawling dark
Drawn on by late December's clock.
To crisp the way to pagan halls
Cloaked (proudly) - in vivid evergreens
Full berried in their reds and whites
That - (in poor light) seem to shimmer cream.

Rime frost - the overture -
Before the show of bleached white snow
Falling cold upon the marrow
Like (fresh laundered) sheet of calico.
Brittle – shapeless – though moulded
To the contours of the ridge and furrow leas -
A stage where high wigged players sway -
Type cast - as looming ash and spreading chestnut trees.

The powder of their wigs -
Lightened by the whirling breeze –
Is tormented by its swirling bight
Then lifted from those brooding trees
To dance - as if for Lucifer
Till let drop – like dross
Onto the flowing river banks -
Shrouded now – in veils of marbled moss.

Rime frost spread out across the piece
Dropped on the dormant tilth -
Bed of leaf fall (hibernation) mulch -
Verges and general roadside filth –
Once bedraggled in their spangled colours
Now chased till out of sight –
Stretching far into the pitch –
Best dressed – in fresh uniform - of white.

Roots

Bare - spindly life lines for trees -
Fibrous tubes referred to as roots -
Providers of support – like feet
Bare - without the protection of boots.

Hidden below life's breathing line
They make their lightless home
In chalk or gravel or the greyest of clay
Or a compost of dark chocolate loam.

Unseen and unheard
Sunk deep down below ground
It is their given task to spend time
In the service of trunk and of crown.

They push up the nourishment needed
For a strong growth of leaves -
Doused by a pesticide protection
From a multitude of parasite thieves.

They grow first young and tender
Ranging through soft to grow hard –
Some bared by the wind -
To expose them - as twisted and gnarled.

Twisted and gnarled these suction straws
Draw trickles of fortitude up to a flow
Juiced with the essence of life
Teased out of the blindness down there - below.

The Route South

I had to get the route map out
To find a place that I might go -
I had planned to visit Lyme
But only got as far as Stow -
Where a part time light on red
Was the start of my despair
For the book had not prepared me for
Such a major road repair.

I sat there for several hours
About as bored as I could be –
I ate a cheese and pickle roll
And drank a flask of aging tea.
A lady crossed in front of me
Muttering something rude –
The butter in my roll was off
And my flask of tea was stewed.

I felt the need to find another route
That would have me on my way -
After all - I perished the thought
Of being stranded there all day.
The traffic news advised we leave
All major roads of dread,
So I took a detour off to Shipston
To get my hair cut there - instead.

My route then took me off -
By back road through to Paxford -
But, due to a navigational error
I motored through to Batsford –
A place where a lady sunbathes,
Though I'm sad to have to say
A young meanie - with scarlet bikini
Was not seen in her hammock all day.

It was then that my car over heated
Discharging a fine head of steam
Causing my engine to boil
And putting a hold on my holiday dream.
I was forced to call for breakdown repair
Explaining my run of bad luck -
At length I was towed to my home
Behind a vehicle recovery truck .

Undaunted by ill fortune I've planned
The route - for my next summer's trip
I thought of a cruise to a place in the news
But didn't fancy a journey by ship.
So I've chosen an overland route
To take me south once again
This time I can't fail – as I'm going by rail -
And leaving the strain to the train.

Rumour

Slowly floating in - as a whisper would
Upon a bitter evening breeze
Drawn - like whistling air through blackened teeth -
I glide among denuded winter trees -
To stand my distance while in watching brief
But for my earnest work to begin
I must now float towards receptive ears
And so flit - a good deal closer in.

Once mouthed I melt the deafening wax -
Clogged ears now hear through oily mist -
Rigid truth slips on slick, wave washed deck -
Thrown by SS fiction's dizzy list.
Ill - or otherwise conceived - once posted I am free -
Un-scotched I must come out -
For sore or good - misunderstood - I'm spread
Like wild fire – far about.

Planted firmly – rooted in that fibrous sponge -
A mischievous but small imagination -
I light upon a reputation - maybe two - of a hapless few
Unfairly - to cause their agitation.
Now I have the smoking green sticks rubbed to life
Hot chatter feeds the boiling jabber mill –
And my smouldering embers find a wind on which to spread
Till cooled - by a truth blown chill.

Searching For Answers

Where does the sun sleep
Before she rises Gran?
In a cot hid in the clouds
High above Japan.

Does she rise late like Dad
And run to catch the bus?
No - the sun keeps perfect time
Each day to shine on us.

Is the sun as strong
As clever people say?
Yes, she lights up all the earth
Turning night-time into day.

How does she know
Where she has to go, Gran?
All can be found, lad,
In God's own master-plan.

Does she have a family
Like we do here on earth?
Yes, she has the planets
Revolving round her girth.

Will she ever leave
For some other sky?
No, she will always stay
And provide rays to light us by.

Does she eat her greens
And meat that's from the bone?
Her food comes from within, lad,
So you see, she makes her own.

Does she clean her teeth
With toothpaste flavoured mint?
Her brightness is her own, lad,
An unpolished giant glint.

Is she young or old?
Does anybody know?
She's as old as time, lad,
Now we really have to go.

Silvered Screen

There steps a well dressed man
Down from a horse drawn tram -
To stride across a shallow void -
Through my home and me,
In his Edwardian urgency
And - by courtesy of my TV
Forewinding a reel of celluloid.

How I would like to speak to him
Step out of mine, into his skin -
Find out where he had slept -
See his breakfast plate -
Find out his lasting fate -
And know if he dallied somewhere till late -
Beguiled by an erotic date he kept?

Suddenly I lurched forward - into the screen
Then - or so it would seem
I was through – through to his time -
A time of horses pulling drays -
Past pan-stick clowns performing plays,
Just a stones throw away from darkened alleyways
Leading to a stench of back street grime.

A half-face stares from a broken pane -
Trapped inside by the sense of shame
That trudges the length of this smoken lane,
With its tenements taken on by rats and mice -
Chesty wheezes - diseases - heads of lice
And daily rounds of human vice -
All confounded by more of the same.

Straining through the half-light
My eyes focused on the plight
Of a street urchin brought to wail
By the sharp cut of a cane -
His fear clearly raised by the pain
While lashed by the soaking evening rain
Come down on a north-east gale.

Coach-horses with eyes rolling white –
Lathering lips curled - as if to bite -
Were trampling – as if to the beat
Of the saddler's endless tap
Splaying rivets into a leather strap
Fashioned out of harness scrap -
To be used to make the hapless bleat.

Then – suddenly – this coarse pandemonium
Was calmed by the Baptist harmonium's
(Barely) audible thankful airs -
Expanded on by the gathering throng
Taking on the congregations song -
A moral verse on right and wrong
To lift those of voice above their worldly cares.

As I stood – shivering - listening there
I thought I saw the silver hair
Of someone I had known in another time
Who – suddenly turned and grabbed me – violently
Hurtling me backwards – through my TV -
Sweating – shaken awake – relieved to be
Back from that place - so different from mine.

Sense of Joy

Elusive – inconclusive – this emotion
Bright as sunlight – grey as cloud
Choked by silence – screamed aloud
This unrelenting - often unfound notion –
Sought diligently – in earnest -
Without sound – cocooned in winter's puss
Though patiently abided - no fuss -
Till brought forth by spring's burlesque.

Amid spring's joy - the nesting farm hen gloats
Over cracking shells of chipping chicks
Who emerge as hen and cockerel mix -
Their gaping beaks – serve as peaks to chasmic throats.
Their screeching – cheeping – greeting
Shows avian gluttons in constant need
Of meal – scraps - cooked peel – to feed
Their greed - spoke loud in urgent screeching.

Quieter though the joy of bud specked thorn -
Bright – vivid – climbing – clean -
Punctuating her black sticks with livid green
Tight curls of piercing – prickled spawn -
Tense – excited – coiled – waiting
For that steepling sunlit cue
To urge them through the glistening dew
And dress the bush in emerald slating.

All now is waking – stretching - flexing
Grass tips – new growth elongating -
Vole – hedgehog - shrew – caught hesitating -
So much to do – so new and so perplexing.
Hungry - hunting - thirsty - quenching
On, once diamond water, now more pliant -
Refreshing tuberous – rooted clients
Of sprouting glade and thorny fencing.

But still elusive - though more conclusive
This emotion - joy - over winter cloud -
Ungagged chatter - called aloud -
An eager breeze spreading her effusive
Nature fest – a spring behest
Repeating last year's grand success -
Without call for joy to acquiesce
To odd discord toward this spring burlesque.

Souls Cocooned

When grown men look towards the sky
They see souls of memories passing by -
Adrift in their puffed-out shrouds
Of dappled grey and off-white clouds.
Seen as reflections in minds of silvered glass
Into which they stare (as grief floats past)
Through eyes closed as they quietly cry -
Letting gossamer tears slip out
For that confusing sky -
Through a flickering - seeping - weeping eye.

Those silvered tears then drip away -
Dissolved by the drying of a day
Tanning weather bleached - redding cheeks -
Sore with salt in tear stain streaks.
Dried – sodium chloride
Left to mark a moment's loss of pride -
Before focus returns once more
To sooth the sores and dull the scars
That had seemed (for a time) so raw
And wipe away such salty hoar.

In the distance – such souls reach the heady beech
Then drop – as if ordained to teach
The thorny fingered hedge to grasp
The unsuspecting fauna - brushing past.
And in return the hedgerow seems to march
From stooping willow to upright larch -
In their burnt green fatigues and berries red -
Straight of line - upright of spine -
As men dream that haws lift rooted boots and tread –
(With care) around - the (long abandoned) osier bed.

Such memories of a life turned mystery -
Conspire to dictate that which they must see -
While soul-laden - cotton wool galleons
Float over battalions of maize seed stallions –
Pointing high towards a misty - lilac sky –
Straining to see where all souls lie
Until they spy a caravan of magic beads -
Blown across the sky like migrant seeds
Or - nomadic spirits - sent to reap
Those souls – that were sown too deep
And left to lie – in an endless keep -
Weeping down below
But - (somehow) leech from under ground
To float – back up to a cumulative sleep.

White Tulips

They bow their cream white heads
To touch the lawn –
Tulips battered with un-seasonable squall
Displayed like virginal pilgrims -
Hooded and forlorn –
Facing the cold stone wall –
Across from
A range of diffident sheds.

April showers – torrential for hours -
Their jewelled droplets bighting -
As ravenous transparent pre-molars -
Grinding on petals of silk -
As though fighting
On the side of spring bloom controllers -
In crushing
All those bowed, cream and white flowers.

Spring bulbs in need of a fling
Colour drained – tear stained
Strained by the bighting eastern drip –
Crying on a breeze - audibly sighing –
As though pained
By a (force eight) Siberian grip -
Snuffing
Out this – one of April's high joys of spring.

Standstill on the M40

Dear Cathy, thanks for arranging our trip to see Ron's play,
The tickets were for the evening, though there was also a matinee.
We were so sorry you couldn't attend, having that awful virus.
Well, we set off in the late afternoon with Ron, there to inspire us.
All went well at first, travelling down from Bourton, through Moreton
And past the Rollright stones, in order to avoid Chipping Norton.
It was on the outskirts of Oxford where we suddenly found
The traffic so heavy that we felt it best to take a detour, round
The tailback, which was caused, at least in our judgment,
By a multi-vehicle crash; resulting in a serious accident.
Faced with this we came to a decision that, as it turned out, made things worse,
As I've recalled and written down in the enclosed verse.
But if you feel our tribulations may cause your stress levels to mount
Just discard my full, though perhaps slightly over elaborate, account.

Well let's move on to more cheerful matters, how are you?
I've heard you've been laid low with the flu and that awful to-do
With poor old Mike, firstly barely able to move with his bad back
And then rushed to hospital with a suspected heart attack.
It must have been a great relief to hear he only has angina
Which I feel, though painful and unpleasant, is just a minor
Problem compared to what might have been the long term effect
Of eating all that bubble and squeak, dripping toast and general neglect.
Still looking on the bright side, Ron is trying to fit us in again for the play,
If there are four unsold tickets available, preferably once more on a Thursday.
He's trying to phone or e-mail the owner, or better still arrange to meet her
So that he can see if she's in agreement, after all it is her theatre.
Well I hope I've managed to cheer you up, at least to some extent,
Because things could be a lot worse, you could be under a slab of cement.

PS. By the way when you rub the goose grease I sent, over your chest,
Remember, it works better if you take off your vest.
Oh! and it's Aunt Maud's funeral next Wednesday so please try
To be there; you know how much you enjoy a good cry.

Still

Impoverished lice - shed
From 'neath the discarded quill -
Let fall from the careless bill
Shredding down - beyond ill -
Mashed into a common swill
Congealed to cold - solidified spill
No longer pliant – far beyond ill -
Crystallized – cold moulded to a porcelain chill
All sound – all spent – fallen still.

Scattered chaff - spread -
Wild winnowed from the silent mill
Down the iced - unmetalled hill -
Ground down – beyond ill.
Mashed into a common swill
Compounded to cold - solidified spill
No longer plastic – far beyond ill -
Crusted – cold-moulded to a porcelain chill
All silent – all spent – all fallen still.

Last remains – last fed
On uncommon – contaminated fill
Existing intestate – without will
Laid down – beyond ill
Mashed into a common swill
Commended to cold – solidified spill
No longer porous – far beyond ill –
Compressed – cold moulded to a porcelain chill
All sound silenced – fallen still.

Stone Faced

Stand alone statues carved as stone representations
Of leaders of nations -
Horse gods with wings - arrogant kings -
Fat aristocrats
Embracing their misbegotten brats -
All authority - all mortality long ago gone
In an epoch of stages -
Through a millennium of ages
To end darkly
In putrefied flesh and grey calcified bone.

Lichen moustaches grow in wet urban green
Over faces once a primmer cream stone
Topping off more than one statue
Of Mark, Luke, John and Matthew
High on their perches
Bedeckers of minsters - cathedrals and churches
Looking down
On the few who punctuate each empty pew
In front of a priest quietly saying
"I've given up praying over such a dispiriting scene."

Sharp edged dictators eroded – dishevelled – mellowed in tone
Chipped cracked and spawling –
Damage appalling
To benefactors misused -
Scarred and bruised by generations of youths
And whether it matters or not,
Spattered with more than a spot of grey pigeon loam
Crowning each head of stone -
Bereft of one thought they could say was their own.
Staring – imperious - silent – alone.

Stormy Dreams

Over the hills they came
Rain and wind together.
Across the valley they rage
Cloud and stormy weather.
Around the plains they whirl
Hail and sleet together.
Over the ground they laid
Snow and winter weather.

Horsemen from the heavens
Battle devils from below.
While ancient fighting galleons
Try to ride the tidal flow.
Battle's fire lights brightly
The night skies from below
And churning volcanic core
Brings lava's molten flow.

Awakened from my sleep
Sweating palms together.
Dreams in cloud a cluster
Dampened by foul weather.
Striking lightning rods with
Thunderbolts fused together.
Over my mind they came
Dreams and stormy weather.

Angels from the heavens
Look down on us below
While Aquarius delivers water
To create the river's flow.
Moonlight sparkles brightly
On irrigation dikes below
And gravitation's spinning joules
Keep up the vital flow.

Into eastern sky they came
Sun rays and dawn together.
Across the fields they scorch
With hot and arid weather.
Melting the roads they boil
Asphalt and tar together.
Around our lives they spread
Bringing in more humid weather.

Strangers Within

Strangers came behind the dark
Unseen by travellers - keen to disembark
From commuter trains now running late
By half an hour- their usual rate
Bringing with them awful squalls
Of drenching water curtain walls
Forming lakes- over drains
Already blocked from recent rains.

Strangers drive in foreign cars
Or stop off to fill our public bars
With their earnest - inane chatter
Naught to do with any parish matter.
Push up prices of our modest homes
Beyond the reach of workmen's loans
Without a thought - no doubt
Of the locals they are putting out.

Strangers move onto our grounds
Pollute our streets with foreign sounds
Create their alien world so near
To the place we hold so dear.
Change the way we run our schools
By introduction of their rules
Restricting what we're allowed to say
With new rules - we must obey.

Strangers who wake us terrified
With the harm they've caused inside
Crass intruders run without control
To leave us fighting less than whole -
Shivering out our chances to forget
As left to drown in ice cold sweat
We ask the darkening emptiness
To turn a light on our distress.

Strangers now have come within
To infect the blood beneath our skin
Our straining hearts pumping them
Around - from top to stem.
These strangers now they treat
But in the end can never beat
For this malady of flowing red
Will not leave till we are dead.

Such Riches

I suppose I was lucky to be left with such riches
As a handleless stocker for cleaning out ditches –
A dull bladed old pocket knife –
And a wealth of worthless advice
That I even tried to act on - once or twice -
Encouraging me to drift my way through life -
Like an old comic cast out to blow
About – (pointlessly) - around in the snow.

An old aunt (who viewed me with affection)
Left me a share in her stamp collection
Which – sadly amounted to so few
That my share (in total) - contained only two.
One had Hitler and a swastika on
That was on a letter sent by my uncle Ron
Which was posted in June '44
Just after he was taken a prisoner of war.

My uncle Jack willed me the slip of his largest ever bet
But the horse lost and I had to clear - his outstanding debt.
He also left me some pea seeds to sow -
(Which I planted) but not one of them grew.
There was also the drink left behind the Red Lion bar
Which (from where I live) is not very far –
But the way my luck ran with him
I didn't feel that I could afford to go in.

My Uncle Fred left me a carved horse and cart
That metamorphosed into a piece of trench art
And a blunt - five eighth masonry drill
Wrapped up in an (unpaid) old utility bill.
There was a blunt pair of pliers
In the saddlebag of a bike with no tyres
He claimed that he had used while in advance
Of the allies - invasion of France.

So I put my lifetime bequests in a sale
For profit where I thought I was bound to prevail –
Till the auctioneer demanded money with an expression so grim
Saying - I was the only vendor owing money to him.
This burden of under achievement -
Brought on mostly by family bereavement -
Has left me with nowhere to go - but to blow
About aimlessly - like a comic cast out in the snow.

Summer's End

The closing clouds of August
Produce their summer play -
As moving shapes and forms
Lit in many shades of grey -
To form a dappled footprint
Of watery colours - painted by
An unknown artist
Against a Wedgwood sky.

Late wisps of reflective cloud
Absorb the faintest burnished tint
Of sunset - turning them to
An iridescent evening pink
Spreading over hedgerows
Ripe in fruit of wild flowers -
Grown thick around the late born sheep
Caught short by autumn's hours.

September sun works less by now
Before she bows and tires
Over lichen slated roofs
And (long shadow) casting spires.
Lowering over weary ploughman
Who scurries cross the barley mow -
From his long day's work
Behind the chisel harrow hoe.

Now rising later – falling sooner -
She sets on early evening dew -
Cools the sap dispensing leaves
To fall as they must do -
Barnacled – black spotted -
Frost burnt wafers over done -
Digested into compost mould
Browned beneath the falling sun.

So the fanciful swallows gather
On the strained electric wires
To sing of going south
By dint of hereditary desires -
So they mill and fall together -
Under-hanging every rooftop perch.
Waiting for their morning call
Expectant - like curates sat in open church.

Then - brightly lit that morning comes
To call all migrants up to swarm -
Circling high - before they fly
South - once more to Capricorn -
And so autumn sets her threat
As clover leaf and stubble blend
Early dew falls where the swallow flew
To start the fall of summer's end.

The Albino Crow

The dirge played on far too long
And wailed to her - too loudly
By a piper sound in breath
Airing his pipes too proudly.
He stood to scourge so long
He froze in a ridged kilted form
Numbed to stiffened bruising
By a wild (Highland) hail storm.

Crashing - fell the chilled marble
Giant, cannonading stones
Large enough to dent a skull
Or shatter finest porcelain bones.

But sadly she was late -
To witness this frenzied frost attack
For she'd stepped in an ice covered puddle
Wearing her grandmother's mac,
From there she sank in a drift
Of soft bleached virgin snow,
Wearing a hat of white feathers
Plucked from the head of an albino crow.

From an idea by L Bell.

Baleful Crow

Oh black bird please tell me
Why do they call you crow?
Do you make a noise at dawn -
Like a cock - with nowhere else to go?

The cock would stay to crow.

Do you chase the hens round,
Then lose them from the pen,
When the fox drags them off
For chicken a la den?

With his vixen a la den.

Oh black bird please tell me
If - like the cock - you fight?
And then loose your chicks -
To a killer from the night?

Owls kill at night.

Swallows swarm in autumn
Because they feel the need to go
So crow - why do you stay?
I would really like to know.

The crow speaks.

"The answers to your questions
Are long and full of woe
So just accept my expression's black
Because I'm a baleful crow."

Indeed - a baleful crow.

The Clinical Way

"Leave the class? – yes, leave the class
Wait outside - don't miss the bus" –
Waiting as ever - shifting – shuffling – pensive –
Loitering - side by side with drying Plantain litter -
Between gaps in waning couch weed grass.

For fourth Monday's chastening flight -
I am brought forward – arranged – not led
There for the clinic –baffled by brightness –
A dark kept – bamboozled lad – confused
Not unknowing – nor yet bright.

Time goes – bus comes – unerringly
A rust and cream tumbrel – half glazed
Laminated with round-eyed ghouls
Staring – recognizing my windows
Through theirs – locked on - unswervingly.

The stodgy driver wriggles to free himself
Belly tyre slaps out from compressing wheel -
He - from helmsman to 'Buddha' baggage boy
Draws me – moistly – stickily inside -
To be sweatily seated beneath the parcel shelf.

They – my unrelated family drool -
For once inside this rattle - metal - packet
I must be Castor – to their painful Pollux -
Unceremoniously oohing and aahing
Their grim overture to a binary ghoul.

My richly deafened ears hear my mind
Call - dash out through bloodied thorn hedge
Where thrush in alder bush ignores my hunger
For sharp exit from this menacing Maria -
Too busy stretching worms to bacon rind.

Narrow by-ways spit out dust or splash -
Then take their turns this way and that
By churns - paint flaking - left to beg?
Bleating flocks and a foreign chimney stack
Ballooning volumes of black pebble dash.

A bursting - stroking pack of pudgy leathered cigars
Spill over the wheel from Buddha's sleeves
Hopping – criss-crossing – occasionally stopping
To animate verbose advice damp with saliva -
Provoked by jumped-up Jacks in their oncoming cars.

Over punctuating cats-eye bumps - we arrive
Spun – dazed - disjointed – glazed -
Sliding over steps of aluminium scree
Greeted by a (scraps from kitchen) smell
And routine 'cargo' check to see if we're alive?

Hands gripped by starched white optician -
Flapping like a dove's last throes of peace
Caught in the grip of flashing tiger's teeth –
His laundered form in slapping uniform
Escorts - we 'accused' to a robotic inquisition.

Memories of trips to the eye clinic as a child (1950's)

The Cricket Season

Whitsun brings our changing ways
Brought on by lengthening of the days
The lighter nights draw us outside
To paddle on a warm spring tide.
Summer pastimes we now support
With the emphasis on pursuing sport -
Pads are cleaned and gloves are found
For practice on the cricket ground.

The pavilion doors thrown open wide
Let fresh air replace the must inside.
Mats are brushed and steps are swept
The beer is tapped and proper kept.
Fresh growing weeds are soon erased
Bare turf patches quick relayed.
Fast growing grass mown off in layers
Fresh prepared for eager players.

The match begins just post midday
With the umpire's shout of ready - play!
The seamer bowls at such a pace
He flies a bouncer past the opener's face.
Then slow left armer with finesse
Turns the match into a game of chess
Between a hopeful century maker
And slow spin bowling wicket taker.

The game is watched by cricket wenches
While old men moan on rustic benches
Curious tourists stand and criticise
The unfathomable sight before their eyes.
Migrating birds here as summer guests
Watch the match from tree top nests.
A blind man comes with his dog to see
If the ladies have begun preparing tea.

The total grows with runs and byes
Interspersed with "owzat" cries
Occasional fours add to the batting cause
Accompanied by polite applause.
The board displays the score - of a sort
Nine wickets down and last man caught.
The final wicket falls to end the runs
And start the race for tea and buns.

After tea it's us who take the middle
To try and solve their batting riddle.
But the visitors seem so assured
As they put us to the willow sword.
Our keeper crouches, perhaps to pray for rain
As the 'leggy' is urged to bowl again.
Though they won for the loss of just one wicket
The way they cheered it's just not cricket!

The Secret Door

There are no traps to trip -
Bring a slip - or cause a fall
Behind the secret door -
Set deep into my garden wall.
Through which I go – to a magic life
Of childhood games -
Played in country lanes –
Criss-crossing a green and buttercupped floor
Just before the outbreak of world war.

A place where my mother's only concerns
Seemed to be (at least to me)
Strawberry jam - the rag and bone man
And we children being late for tea –
Sunburn on our arms and legs -
The gypsy woman selling pegs -
Weaning piglets – old sows giblets
And produce from the filling earth
Swelling granddad's bulbous girth.

Where I felt the cars were real
And I find myself behind the wheel
Of a Morgan flier
Built of ash - with spokes of wire.
An open top (as the hood is down)
The wind in my hair as I speed to town
With Hilary Brea and Alison Grey
(Who both agreed to be my date that day.)

And then to my delight -
I met Biggles - as evening waited for night.
He tells me that Ginger's ill
And he would like me to fill
The vacant place - (of course I will)
In one of his fighter-pilot seats
And to join him - as they race -
Up at a pace – as if intent on outer space.

We practiced with mock attacks
Crawling across Luftwaffe backs -
Diving from the setting sun
To end the fight - almost before it had begun.
What a way to stay and play
In a world of every colour
Except (that is) dull grey –
Or fawn – or bay
Helping Biggles - (even if for only – one part day).

The Crimson Coach

A youth at a cross-roads stood,
Not knowing which way was right
When a crimson coach came - lit
From somewhere in the night.
As the coach drew to a halt
The boy could clearly see inside
Where a single traveller smiled -
While offering him a ride.

The oil lamps blazed brightly
Both inside the coach and out -
To light upon such splendour
Only great wealth could bring about.
Upholstered - fixtures and fittings
All padded in crimson red
And - like matched heavy cushions
Sewn - with silk and satin thread.

"I fear I can not afford to ride".
Said the lad with envy cords
Tightly strangling his reply
By wrapping hard round his words.
"Your livery and high bred horses
Are beyond any way I might match their cost
So I must sorely walk apace
To find the way that I have lost."

The man leant on decorated arms -
Elbows propped on finely tailored knees -
Replying that the ride was free
To take - or leave - as he might please.
The carriage was full heated
Against the winter's bight
And the seats were set for rest
Bathed in the palest amber light.

As the cold found his marrow
Now freezing in his bones -
The air was filled with mongrel's yelp
And haunting tinker's groans.
His belly gurgled in a loud distress
No mother could bear to hear
And so – closed by such dark company
He stepped into his coming fear.

The door shut (tight) upon his past
Of good family and old friends
And the rarest differings of folk -
Those always quick to make amends.
Gone the company of jolly men
And the joy of maidens' hearts
As the crimson coach careered
To a castle filled with blacker arts.

He was shown to the comforts
Of a room done out blood red
With steaming mineral water tub
And the softest feather bed.
But he was soon to discover
That he would have to beg -
To have the unseen shackle
Removed - from about his leg.

Then he gave to his new master -
(By deceit), his mortal soul
To be cut from truth and cast
Into Lucifer's dark bowl.
Where a black serpent bit -
Into his last vestige of worth -
Paralyzing his unheard words –
From any hearing on the Earth.

The Deity of Joy and Gaiety

My God - would be in charge of leisure
Manifested as – the Minister for pleasure –
He would (of course) need staff
To run the show - on his behalf –
Two cherubs would be hired
Named good Ribaldry and Panache –
The former to take things seriously
And the second -
There only - to launder all his ill begotten cash.

The only fruit allowed would be modified
Soaked in syrup and then canned
And rice and boiled fish diets would most certainly be banned.
He'd fine anyone found eating porridge
And pay for dripping toast to be encouraged –
A reversal of the practice of - the paying of demurrage.
Vegetarians would be offered tax breaks
If they would all agree to eat
A daily pound or two - of fatty lumps of reddish meat.

And brothels –be advised
Would – be (quickly) legalised.
Where majorette band drummers
Would seduce any innocent –
Wassailing - young country bumpkin Mummers -
Apprentice carpenters and plumbers.
Whether it be winter or mid-summer –
While dairy farmers would all get their rightful fill.
There - in their rustic (milking maid) idyll
Without having to travel miles -from their local cider mill.

Smokers would be deemed a special case
Black Rod would carry spliffs (ready rolled) inside his mace
And as a compliment to this -
Pipe tobacco would all be cut – with blocks of cannabis.
Cigars would be issued free
To every purchaser of a new – (petrol guzzling) car -
But unfortunately still only allowed
To be lit - in any one of those new sheep pens
Currently springing up - all around our public bars.

If you should choose to write to him
Please allow time for his reply
For he's not been well of late – with so much upon his plate -
Ribaldry is of the opinion that it could be -
Something that he sniffed or even that he ate –
Oh and please sign yourself as a willing member of his laity
And address your dear missive to the 'Deity of Joy and Gaiety'.

The Duty Field

Blank fields do not cultivate themselves
Human steam must open up the valves
That till and load the storehouse shelves.

Each morning bringing ever greater toil
To spread enrichment on the soil
So winter planted crops don't spoil.

Hard labour for those good peasants willing
And those called on to spray for killing
Off pests - bent on the ruin of weeks of tilling.

For the sun in June's sky is warming
Wasp and hornet larvae forming -
Imago plagues of insects swarming.

While germinating seeds show sprout
Through the dust of July's long drought -
Calming - farming people's frenzied doubt.

Each earnest husbander and willing mate
Working through long hot days till late -
To raise fresh crops for dining plate.

No breaks for rest are taken here
Because of underlying fear,
That famine could rule the coming year.

So cutting and thrashing must be done -
Late picking of apple, pear and plum -
Pickling crops, soused in briny drum
Must be complete before bleak winter's come.

The Golden Cider Jar

So - urgent now is the search to find the cider jar
That first fell still upon the flagstone floor,
Long since put upon the shelf - too high by far.

Parched they were - as many people often are
With nought but water left to stem their gore,
So - urgent now is the search to find the cider jar.

Found only were dry cups stained as treacle tar
So now they seek that golden jar once more
Long since put upon the shelf - too high by far.

Desperate were they by now to find a licensed bar
Which - when found was closed by act of war
So - urgent now is the search to find the cider jar.

There was n'er a choice 'twix apple juice and char
So needed now - the jug that propped the open door
Long since put upon the shelf - too high by far.

Their search is now set to music from an old guitar
But still they find no juice from pulp and core
So - urgent now is the search to find the cider jar
Long since put upon the shelf - too high by far.

The Herefordshire Clun

Herefordshire was conquered
By Edward the Black Hill ram
Who divided up the land
To be grazed by English lamb.
His pal Offa, the upper Clun
Was told to dig a dyke so deep
It would help with law and order
And keep out marauding sheep.

Then a flock of Ba-Barbarians
Crept in with blackened face
Led by Glen, a Scottish ram
Who took over Edward's place -
Gripping his short and curlies
From Shropshire down to Ross
Now Edward's in a stew
And Glen's the Woolly Boss.

Glen staked his claim for land
When he drew the Mapa Mundi
Starting one wet Saturday
And finishing a week on Sunday.
He drove out the Herdwicks
Then set upon a thorough search
To find out which were Jacob's
And put them in the church.

Now some may seek revenge -
So when mixing with the locals
Be careful how you speak
To those black faced curly yokels.
Always be prepared to leave
If there's even the merest hint
Of the sharpening of carving knives
Or the chopping up of mint.

So! great care must be taken
When travelling through to Wales,
For though sheep show their wool
Some folk could be hiding ovine tails
Because inter-breading it was rife
Once they discovered wellies
During that time between the wars -
Before they were given tellies.

The Hurrying Storm

A wild wind stalked the rising hill
To cast her Arctic chill
Into the warm surround of the water powered mill

To shake the rattling door and window pane,
Band saw and revolving plane
Before she turned - to breeze her way back out again.

The damage done was sore but of little cost -
With no cutting lost
Just working fingers stiffened by the chill of winter frost

While those penetrating eyes of crafty damp
Seized the gripping clamp
And watered down the light - spilt from flicker lamp.

Sawdust choked out from mouths - to form a woody gore
Freed once more
To return again as a (sputum mix) upon the creaking floor.

Her brash whistling hound threw loosely rooted crops,
Resting brooms and mops
Over leaning break of trees and wall of hedgerow tops.

Barrels chased after cattle with their calves in tow
Skittered by the north east blow -
Trampling down a meadow - set aside as winter mow.

So was sent a squall to wash the rabbit to her fate -
Start the dance of roofing slate
To the ever drumming dirge of a (banging) iron gate.

Deadened echoes of a thousand mothers' distant calls
To young washed from nursery halls
And swept on – to cascade over (flash flood) waterfalls

While pecking game - with one cocked weather eye
Have their feathers ruffled by
The flailing arms and legs of havoc wheeling from the sky.

So the tempest's wrath came crashing down
And caused much life to drown
In flattened field - fledgling wood and battered town.

The Judgement

T'was a bad day for our town
When the Squire was knocked down.
'E'd just stepped out from the door
Of 'is 'ansome, gilded coach and four.
When 'e slipped beneath the wheel
After returnin' from a banquet meal.
Upon which, 'is coachman drove away
With all three bays and a gelded grey.

There was talk of a murder charge,
Which I felt was rather 'arsh,
Well, the Squire, he wasn't dead
So 'e was charged with homicide instead.
The trial was somewhat unfair
'Cos the coachman wasn't there
And the Squire 'ad left 'is private ward
For foreign parts - abroad.

We understands the coachman's wife,
When he got sent down for life,
Asking for government support.
Giving as her reasons to the court,
"I support five children of my own,
Two strays and one on loan.
My father and his mother
And the milkman's younger brother."

Lord Chief Justice Keyte
Said "we recognise your plight
So, if you withdraw your bold request
We will give your husband best.
But when we release him from his cell,
He must apologise as well
As leave at the break of day
To do some time in Botany Bay."

What else was there for 'im to do
'E'd 'ave to sail as a member of the crew.
They 'ad reached 'alf way down to Spain
When the ship was sunk, by 'eavy rain.
The news soon reached our town
Which brought a melancholy down,
'Cos 'e'd bin pardoned out of 'and
To do with bein' leader of our band.

You can imagine our surprise
When the coachman returned - alive,
With base trombone, an' cornet
'E'd rescued from the M.V. Hornet.
The child they 'ad on loan
Could play the slide trombone
An' the cornet comes to life
At the lips of the coachman's wife.

We celebrated at the annual show
With the band a playin' at full blow.
There was children's donkey rides,
Cricket played, as six-a-sides,
Stalls with some very good buys,
Old fashioned coconut shys,
An!' some game, which several played,
Involvin' a dark haired kitchen maid.

You can imagine 'ow it took our breath
When we 'eard of the Squire's early death.
The body was then brought back
Wrapped in paper, an' a 'essian sack.
For 'e was poor, without 'is cash
All of it lost in the Wall Street crash.
But 'is interment was already planned,
A procession, lead by the parish band.

Over the grave a solo trumpet played
The tune, "all debts weighed an' paid"
The coachman made a movin' speech
About the Squire bein' out of reach.
Then blew on 'is trumpet, a merry a glee
Called, "joy to the space left by thee."
The coachman's sadness was 'ard to tell,
T'was 'id behind 'is smile so well.

The Kiosk

There stood the box full glazed and red
Set slightly back from a grassy sea -
A verge sprayed over in clover
Cut beneath an aging sumac tree.

This box of telecommunication
Planted there to set our voices free -
Had a chromed and spinning dial
And two buttons - marked with 'A' and 'B'.

We members of the ragged trouser faith
Wondered who had chosen such a place
To build this tiny talking house - perhaps
It had fallen here – from deep in outer space.

But Billy's granddad said it had arrived
Some years before the second war
To trap we unruly truant boys
And give them women folk another means to jaw.

But there was more to this than met the eye
For it could 'call a person up' when all alone
Which brought we wondernaughts to see
This was – 'a truly magic - telephone'.

The Midnight Boat

The Irish Sea stood as if on end -
A churning morass - boiling
Like melted bottles - seen
Drawn from an endless spoil heap
And disturbed as a fearful green
Thrashing water movement - gone deep
Into an unorchestrated rage
Like unpractised dancers – stood on a heaving stage.

With the author's once bright candles gone -
Spluttered out and drowned
In an anger, without fashion,
Banished to a boiling hell
Of savagery without compassion
Haunted by death's chilling knell -
Once heard by drowning sailors
Thrown from decks of capsized whalers.

Hearts – heavy in the storm
Are only steadied
By the throbbing diesel screw
Slowly pushing us across
This oil spattered cold green stew
That threatens growing loss
With spits of surf blown off the sea
To fill those gasping throats with a blistering scree.

From rusty stem to sagging stern
This ocean going bronco bucks -
As if to toss both poor and fine
Greening cowboys from the scrum
And cast them to a curdling shrine -
As their slender holds are perished - numb
Upon the oxidizing fore-deck rail -
With only seconds now till the last grips fail.

But though white knuckles are unclenched
Beneath sickly faces - turned inward
By the groaning carrier's pitch and yaw -
None are launched into the briny slip
That dries ghostly on the pallid jaw
Burning those bloodless lips
Who wish to roar into the mist - "No more"
Just set us firmly down - on Ellan Vannin's shore.

The Missing Cider

August was the month
I remember as a lad
We was 'alf way through when
The weather started turnin' bad.
The temperature 'ad dropped
An' it was feelin' somewhat thin
So we thought we ought
To start an' get the 'arvest in.

We 'ad to do our work
Most days in greatest earnest
Cos the gaffer 'e 'ad bin sent
To do some jury service.
All was a workin' there by five
On the reaper an' the binder,
Though there was some as was
In need of a sharp reminder.

Over near a couple of weeks
All was safely gathered in
So we'd impress the gaffer
By a pleasantly surprisin' 'im.
For we could work just as well
When 'is absence wasn't even there
With all 'is puffin' an' 'is blowin'-
Which of course was just hot air.

The barn was filled to burstin'
Though they bales did seem slightly green -
Still t'was a wondrous sight
Best any of us 'ad ever seen.
A week or so 'ad gone by
When Ol' Barker started showin'
Just where it was 'e reckoned
They bales 'ad startin' glowin'

I could ‘ear Old Barker clearly -
’cos ’e was a freely shoutin’ out -
So I asked ‘im to explain
What ’is noise was all about.
But ‘e just did carry on
To rant an’ shout an’ cus -
Well! ‘e ‘adn’t bin proper schooled
As ’ad bin the rest of us.

The barn ‘e said was very ‘ot
An’ could cause a sorry plight
If we wasn’t very careful
The whole thing could set alight.
Well ‘is timin’ was unfortunate -
A givin’ forth in the Ruddy Duck at night -
Though we did all give ’im best when on returnin’
To see the barn a burnin’ very bright.

So we got quickly to the task
Of a stoppin’ the fire gettin’ any wus
’elped by ’alf the Fire Brigade
Who was in the pub with us.
The engine quickly followed
An’ was not givin’ any quarter -
Till we ‘it a sort of snag
By a runnin’ short of water.

There was nothin' else to do
But break them cider barrel tops
An' pour that precious apple juice
On them fierce burnin' crops.
Well it took all they fifty barrels
To suffocate that fiery blaze
A leavin' all of us a gaspin'
In an unquenched thirsty haze.

The moanin' got so loud
We was all quite sore disturbed
'Til we found part of the noise
Was from an injury just occurred.
For there 'ad bin the sharpest crack
When Ol' Barker slipped an' broke 'is leg
Which we splinted up with binder twine
Wound round a settin' peg.

I explained to the gaffer
'Ow we 'ad saved the rick
Though of course we'd lost the barn
An' 'ad one man gone off sick.
'E looked a bit dis-spirited
At what 'ad bin a gonin' on
But to be fair - 'is main concern
Was, 'where 'ad all the cider gone?'

Through the Butcher's Window

Through the butcher's window
There's beef the best in show.
Legs of young spring lamb
And home cured boiling ham.
Chickens from the deep freeze
Faggots best to eat with peas.
And sheep's cutlets laid out by row
Through the butcher's window.

Through the butcher's window
I see all the things I know.
Stewing steak roughly diced
Streaky bacon clearly priced.
Braising liver for all to try
Kidneys there to fill a pie.
Steak that's felt the hammer blow
Through the butcher's window.

Through the butcher's window
I can see someone I know.
She's buying gammon slices
They're on sale at special prices.
Then there's Old Man Maggotts
Just bought half a dozen faggots -
One's dropped on to the floor below.
Through the butcher's window.

Through the butcher's window
I look to and fro
Meat hangs from every straining rack
Or stacked on shelves near to the back.
There are whole lamb's legs
Next to freshly laid farmyard eggs.
And scraps that help his dog to grow
Through the butcher's window.

Through the butcher's window
That's as far as I can go.
I'd like to be removing tags
Putting meat in shopping bags.
I'd like to buy that piece of brisket
Underneath the ten bob ticket.
But can't afford a scrawny rabbit - so
I just stand there and stare –
Through the butcher's window.

The Poacher

The poacher crept on drying grass,
Then hid to let the keepers pass,
Behind ash trees still thick with keys
Not yet blown by autumn breeze.
Now the silence coming to his ear
Tells him that the coast is clear.
He can see the snare - set over there -
Has caught a dashing, half-grown hare.

He keeps as low as he can be
By moving slow on hand and knee.
To prevent alarm upon the farm
And reduce the risk of bringing harm.
But as he reaches for his prize
He is caught by a chill surprise.
Through a gap - an arresting chap
Springs on him the keeper's trap.

At dawn the poacher, under key and lock
Is dragged into the courtroom dock.
The Beak says he will hear the plea
That he expects to be one of guilty.
The prisoner states, " I've shot not one,
And the keepers they were blinded by the sun."
But the court had little time for pantomime
And fined him twenty shillings for the crime.

An uncle, visiting from another county
Was called upon to pay the bounty.
But he had not the fee to set his nephew free
So left him to fall on the Bench's mercy.
"If you fail to produce the bond or bail"
The beak said "you must go to jail.
And as the fine's missing this court is risen -
And you - my ill begotten man - will go prison."

The sun shone bringing weather fine
As prisoners walked chained to the line.
Then sudden rain brought unexpected gain
For the wet let slip the poacher from his chain.
Not one officer seemed to see
The poacher, once again, drop to his knee.
Rolling down the grade of grassy blade
Was how the poacher's break was made.

Once in the woods he new so well
There was no way the Cops could tell
Of his ins and outs and whereabouts
So they gave in to their niggling doubts.
When they arrived at the prison gate
They had to explain why they were late.
Reporting to the boss one prisoner lost
For which they had to pay the cost.

Once more free he grew in fame
By taking more of the gentry's game.
He oft caught conies half as big as ponies
And sold them to some Guiting cronies.
Pheasant moved from off the land
Past them keepers with some slight of hand -
Though squire lead they were too well fed
To stand any chance of catchin' foxy Fred.

The Raven

The raven flies against the sky
And oversees the crouching pedestry –
Formed by those slow moving – crawling –
Those straining ungainly in their hauling
Of earthbound burdens to and fro
As if unsure which way to go –
Unstopping – uncropping – bound
And tethered - to the unforgiving ground.

While he stays winging at a pace
As if in airborne chase
Of lesser crows – caught hiding
And brought out for his lordly chiding,
Poured on all those puffings and blowings
Done by larks found crowing
And crows found larking -
With his shrill, but strangely melodic barking.

Or soaring over finialed towers
Through bright sun and dull showers -
With time to take a casual rest
And show a steady rise of interest
In the crabbing of paddled boats
Wrapped and roped in addled floats -
At which he might be drawn to gloat
While preening, his black fluorescent overcoat.

Widely he sees as clearly his mind
Unravels the machinations of rushing mankind
Striving for something in which they believe
But unaware they chase what they can not achieve -
As they become evermore becalmed –
Uncharmed by traffic chaos – though irrevocably harmed
By the relentless hustle and bustle done day on day -
While the raven spreads his wings and flies away.

The Reading

The congregation was hushed -
Bowed - with an air of finality.
The hankies were out
And I was in some doubt
That those tears could be shed for me.

But with the tributes read
The prayers were then said.
Said to set the spirit free -
But as they were mouthed
A cold shiver said they were for me.

A bugle blew a rousing tune.
A tune that could not be -
For it sounded the last post
In honour of my ghost -
How could a bugle be sounding for me?

The drummer struck a marching beat
A beat that's meant for soldiers' feet
Off to a war for the cause of liberty.
But when I heard those sombre drums
I knew they were beating for me.

When the body was lowered down
It was clear for all to see -
That as the mourners turned away
Those tossed handfuls of clay
Had been scattered over me.

Once the gathering was fed
And codicils and will were read,
The bank trustee took out his fee
As a division on the property -
That once belonged to me.

So I wait with little grace
Between Heaven and purgatory -
Until I'm called to put my case
And hope they offer a space
In a place that feels welcome to me.

Robins and Eggs

A robin came this morning
But unlike the rhyme
Doesn't seem to have the time
To stop and speak to me.
He seems perplexed
Perhaps his mate
Is flying in late
For their date - in the apple tree.

Meanwhile - through the window,
If I'm not mistaken
Wafts the smell of eggs and bacon
Sizzling in the pan.
The smell of coffee beans
Ground and roasted
Buttered crumpets lightly toasted -
Done to feed the inner man.

But I will have to starve
Because those breakfast smells
Come from down at number twelve -
I suppose I knew it all along.
And the robin's flown
Without so much as a beg your pardon -
Into next door's garden -
Something must be wrong.

Ah! there's the robin hen
Behaving in a girly way
That could make the robin's day
Now she's in the breeding mood.
But the robin's courtship
Doesn't help to quell
Those desires I feel as well -
The hunger pangs for food.

So my empty pains dictate
That I leave my perch
And go in search
Of food to break my fast.
But I return with not one single crumb
While the robins feed
And then start to breed -
Without a thought for my ill repast.

Thoughtless Sorts

A battery of thoughtless sorts
Come as regular invaders to our shore
I wish they'd turn straight round again
And go back - to the place they were before.
It won't be very long now - you'll see
Till most are invited here to stay -
Making our lives the poorer -
Because it's us who'll have to pay.

They'll join the swelling throng
And vanish into an ever deepening mist
A few – I suppose - will stay sober
While most – no doubt – will gain a bit of a list -
Brought on by those alco-pop things
And a 'lake full' of lager and bitter.
They'll eat tons of greasy McDonalds and chips
And then scar our proud streets with their litter.

The scandal is the likes of me have no work
Because we're white – heterosexual and male.
The clerk on the desk said, "I could have got you in -
If only you'd been just a little less pale".
Gone are the days when your complaint
Went to the blighters - direct
Now they hide behind official directives
And shaft you - while staying politically correct.

They say they will issue us all with identity cards
Then our concerns will at last be addressed
Though these new powers will in no way be racist
'cause each registration will be the same as the rest.
They say this may infringe on our privacy
And cause exasperation to most peoples senses -
But - they'll catch more license evaders
And increase convictions for parking offences.

They've taken the police from out of their cars
But sadly - have not put them back on their bikes.
They're too busy detaining those immigrant types
But not to worry – it's only the ones we don't like.
Oh! and now there are going to be many more doctors -
I've heard every Tesco will be issued with one.
You can shop - while you wait for a health check -
All day – they're calling it healthcare – 'With Fun.'

Travelling Time

We 'ad t' goo to Laverton
A fow miles this side o' Staverton
You could a sin it on a sunny day
'Sept the 'ills gets in the way
Gaffer said you'll 'af t' walk
At least as far as Weston fork
I decided I ud thumb a lift
With the milkmon early shift.

Ol' Pecker 'ad set out to cycle
Just t' please the gaffer Michael,
When 'e remembered at Paul's Pike
'E'd left 'ome without 'is bike.
'E gev 'is Woodbine a extra drag
Hiccuped twice a swollerin' down the fag.
'E next turned red an' gev a cough
'It the curb an' then fell off.

Ol' Bert was on the back of a lorry
A gooin' up past Featherstun's Quarry
When the wheel went over a spike
In avoidin' a pre-war motorbike.
This caused the tyre to deflate
An' ol' Bert a bein' late.
'E shot up the scaffold to the crown
Through the plank an' stret back down.

They 'ad t' 'ave a fow days off
Them not fit t' spit nor cough.
So I spent some time a peelin'
Paper from the church room's ceilin'
With Fred Bennett, lead light maker
An' sometimes a wager taker.
Fred fancied bein' the Legion keeper
'Cos the beer in there was cheaper.

Ol' Pecker had some close call
When 'e took 'is Paul's Pike fall
From the bike of next door's wife
Which could 'ave easily saved 'is life.
With no crossbar to entangle
'Is wotsit's round, like a mangle
So 'e'll soon be back amongst the men
If 'e don't get lost again.

They was both sun back on site
An' Pecker 'ad to paint the winders white.
Bert said "Pecker you've let me down"
"You've put the paint on upside down"
Pecker chuckled back at Bert
"Jokes like that ull never work
Your 'umour's a wearin' very thin
'Cos I've read the label on the tin"

The customer gev Pecker quite a fright
She wanted the doors in black and white
He moaned, "these folk be funny types
Where can y' get paint! with stripes?"
"You needs pianner paint," sez Fred,
"I got a tin in the back o' me shed.
I won't charge I can see your plight
Just buy me a pint in the Bell's tonight."

Pecker buys Fred a glass o' stout
An' thanks 'im greatly for 'elpin' out
Monday mornin' Fred gives the tin
T' Pecker an' sez "apply it thick an' thin"
Pecker returned an' 'ad t' stress
To ol' Fred it was a mess.
"Well" sez Fred, "you got it free
An' it makes a mess, the same for me"

Trunker's Left

Trunker 'arris- so they tells me
'as left the Volunteer.
I finds it 'ard to swallow -
This news I'm sad to 'ear.
For it was 'im as started up again
When Whitbreads turned it in,
By a servin' Baptists ale
An' showin' Catholics 'ow to sin.

'e took on a girl called Di
An' a lad they called Big Mac
An' then for a year or two
'e 'ad Aunt Sally down the back.
'is missus was in the kitchen
An' in the bar as well.
I think that she was overworked,
'earin' of the 'ardships she did tell.

O' course 'e made many changes
With two rooms turned into one
An' then 'e removed the lid'ole
Where ower drinkin' 'ad begun.
The bar billiards table disappeared
To where - I can not say
But at least I a'nt knocked a skittle down
Since we've 'ad no where to play.

'e started bed and breakfast
For them as 'ad come from off afar,
'e put a pipe into the brook
Then put 'is own brew upon the bar.
'e started up a cribbage team
In which 'e played an' lost a few
But alus claimed 'e could a won -
If 'e 'ad wanted to.

'e put 'is 'eart an' soul in
To 'im it was "is life
An' only ever broke from work
When 'e 'ad to bath the wife.
Many women wished to sleep with 'im,
t'was 'im as told me so -
But 'e 'ad no thought for such affairs
So t'wasn't that as caused 'is legs t' bow.

'e 'ad to see a specialist
About the problem with 'is walkin'
An' whilst 'e was sat in there
'e an' the doctor they got talkin'.
Trunker said, "I would be grateful
If - when you've cured me knees
You could p'raps - arrange
To change me glasses please?"

Well - I bin off on me travels
An' 'ave just returned of late
To 'ear this shockin' news
Of ol' Trunker an 'is fate.
I was sad to 'ear that 'e 'ad left,
Which of course would be 'is right
An' that 'e plans to not return -
But then again they sez 'e might.

But things be not so bad
For them new girls be decent folk
An' the gaffer Keith - it seems to me
Be a very pleasant bloke.
An' some things they 'aven't changed -
By a stayin' the same so far.
An' one of these I'm glad to see
Be young Di – still a stickin' out -
From 'er place behind the bar.

Unavoidably Detained

Late and cold and stranded
By those callous planner's underhanded
Disregard for our need to flow
Without halt - or cause to slow.
Being held against our will
Lurching down from slow to still -
Unwilling and un-replete -
Restrained in ever hardening seat.

Trapped in the bowels of a metal snake
Forced to ride the clutch and brake -
Stalled in our manic rush
To circumnavigate the crush –
Bunting – shunting head to tail
Going nowhere on an asphalt rail -
Of over-crowding front to back -
In darker mood than midnight black.

The night unwinds the time away
Too late now - to see the play -
Or for chance to catch the Delhi flight
As we all grow sick of the sight
Of our new friend's rear bumper -
His wife's garish Christmas jumper –
The fluorescent bikers sneaking through
And a growing need to use the loo.

Conversation becomes so hard
As we measure progress by the yard -
The jokes have turned from flat to sour
By the time we end the second hour.
The second hour out of three
Of our low unwarranted misery
Interred in that snake of breaking red -
Exhausting fumes and cooling tyre tread.

Three hours before we are out -
A further quarter on the round-a-bout
Before we hear the engine roar
With the throttle pushed down to the floor.
No respite for the break horse power
As we return within the hour -
Alighting into the welcome night
With hugs and smiles of sheer delight.

Visiting Memories

The old cottage home,
Derelict and shabby stood -
A sadly dampened shell -
Near to the path into the wood.
The oaken gate has gone,
Though her sturdy posts remain -
Now hung with steel replacement -
Secured by heavy lock and chain.

Her walls of warm rough brick,
Hand made in russet red -
Cast an early evening shadow
Over the old petunia bed.
Some gilly flowers still survive
Dressed in fading petals -
Though long since conquered
By invading thorns and nettles.

An April sun brought memories
Of the mistress - with head bare,
When a gust took off the navy hat
Which she always seemed to wear.
Followed by a shaft of sunlight
Which caught her unaware -
As the wind blew out a silver comb
From her tangled greying hair.

From these old memories I woke
Returning from a distance past -
For the sun had now made way
To dark clouds - come overcast
With drops of early winter rain
That always seems to know
When it is the perfect time -
For them to turn to snow.

The snow dances freely down -
Twisting round in ever tighter curls
Floating through the cooling air
Like spinning frosted pearls -
To quickly form a blanket
Over fresh dug turn and fold -
Each flake caught in silvered light
To turn to endless hues of gold.

The darkness fell so silently
On the cottage and her grounds -
I'll swear I saw a keeper
Going on his rounds.
His head was slightly cocked
His cap was set to port
And his striding gait was stretched
To see those poachers caught.

I blink - then stare again
Across the waltzing snow -
Hoping that my mind will let
Tonight's sad nostalgia go -
For with daybreak comes reality -
As I return along this road
With a dozen demolition men
To bring down my old abode.

Walking the Way

Passing by the osier beds
I see old women leaving -
Armed with twigs enough
To carry on their weaving -
Making pots and pecks
And wicker carboy caskets -
Twelve pound chips and trugs
And high class picnic baskets.

Then briskly up to Dyer's lane
Edged by the bluebell wood
And hedges in the green
Of late spring's newing bud.
Overhead a kestrel flies
As if a stringless dancing kite
Or a single seated glider
Set on a thermaled flight.

I take the hill onto the gallops
Where some ewes are laying -
Watching - where nearby
Late born lambs are playing -
Near a shading march of limes
Where a rise of spiteful thistles stay
Sharp - bristling - prickles set
To corrupt the sweetening hay.

A short pace out to sunlight,
Before the turning of an hour
Where I'm pleased to face
The waiting Broadway Tower.
Walking on - through a foot
Of quickly growing wheat
Near a weight of walkers
On a wall - adopted as a seat.

By the road out to my right
Grows a crèche of poppy weeds
Sown by a late autumn gust
Dusting all in a richness of seeds.
Across the road the flat field
Leads me over Fish Hill
Where I stop for a brief moment
To robe against the brewing chill.

On - through the wood
Having dodged the traffic flow -
I stride onto hill grazing
With but a few strides left to go.
Taking on the final slope -
With dips from scarp to steep -
I come across a frolic of lambs
In no hurry to be sheep.

The view is worth the walk -
Across Malvern into Wales
But then it starts to rain
In fact it turns to hail.
I make my way to shelter
Waiting near the tower door -
Just until the rain stops
And sun appears once more.

I punctuate my rest
With fresh cut bread and cheese,
Amid fellow picnic makers
Drinking squash or steaming teas.
Then take my rooftop view
And having seen I go back down.
To take one final look before
I return to Campden Town.

Warrior Brave

Brave - they said of me
But no words could cure the ache
For the chill death circumstance
That each night kept me awake
Arms and legs that searched
For bodies never found
Refused to leave my drumming head
To rest in peaceful ground.

Fight - they said to me
Against the tank and infantry
Of Turk and Johnny Serb
To bring (quick) victory.
Fix your Sheffield bayonet
And run their black hearts through
Give those Balcaneers the steel
That is their coming due.

Charge - they said to me
Leave your resting bench
Take with you a gallant few
From that stinking trench -
Towards the baying enemy
Who chant 'You die in bed'
Cut short their curdling taunts
And send them to hell instead.

Fire - they said to me
And blow an awesome gap
Between his whiskered chin
And the poke upon his cap.
But my powder it was damp
And my bullet was not true
So his return took out my life
When my blood he drew.

Tall they said of me
Standing six feet four
That was the height of me -
Before I went to war.
But now in height we're all the same
Lay in an unmarked grave -
Blasted torsos that were once -
Said to be so brave!

Western Style Democracy

A conversation between Tony Blair and Robin Cook

Our intelligence reports are quite plain
We have no option but war with Saddam Hussein
He has vast piles of W.M.D
On this matter – I simply ask that you should trust me.

I'm sorry Tony I don't see all those weapons you seem to see
And to invasion without the UN – I simply cannot agree.

O.K., I accept regime change is not a good reason to fight
Of course it's illegal and therefore - wouldn't be right
But his weapons still remain hidden – well until
We seek them out – and of that I'm certain we will.

But it's quite clear – this UN amendment hasn't just been made
So that you and your American friends are free to go and invade.

Look – he's been messing us all about
He's even thrown the UN's inspectors out
When clearly it was right that they should remain -
The President and I have made this perfectly plain.

Surely Tony – though it goes against the grain
You have to accept that he's finally let them in again.

This latest charade simply proves what we've always been saying
It's just more of the brinkmanship that he's always been playing -
So now it's time to go to war - with our policy of shock and awe
In order for us to restore – a 'western style' democracy - in Iraq once more.

I must make clear Tony – that I believe this to be an illegal invasion
Which you and George Bush are about to force onto a sovereign nation.

Look – OK if there's no W.M.D our cause will be even greater
Because – at least we will have freed Iraq from an evil dictator –
Of course we accept that a great many lives will be lost
But war's a bloody business in which there will always be some human cost.

Then I resign – in protest against shedding British blood over Iraqi soil –
Just to satisfy your giant ego and their insatiable demand for oil.

Yellow Church

Ill lit pinnacle -
Sighting through the dark -
Waiting - for in-coming fire?
Not known.
Seen clear in cold form
By those who do not enter there -
At her Mass -
But in black - as mourning
Drawing those who clamour prayer
Within her 'midnight' crypt.
To them sanctuary -
Though to those exposed -
Only gaunt roost to mauve pigeon -
Fleck starling or black crow.

Black Shoes

Blue rinse, chocolate mink,
Worn over a white bodice of lace
Edged in pink ribbon
Above a pleated, charcoal skirt.
Seamed fishnet legs
Stride, over patent leather shoes
Polished high to glow
More brightly - than the Devil's own crow.

Grey Pan

Bald bacon kissed the pan
To fry – in rosemary of lard,
Eggs of tangerine and chalk
Cooked - like giant daisy roundels -
Sausages pricked to sizzle out
In this vat of scalding fat.
Fresh - half sliced - a red tomato's pate
Brings welling juices to salivating palate
Upon a willow patterned plate.

All scraps boiled down
To feed the fattened cock
Putting on a courtship show -
But not a fallen scrap -
For the hollow bellied crow.

Yubberton and Paxford Home Guard

Last Friday I met a lad
I calls Ashley - cos it be 'is name.
'e'd just come from the pub –
Well - 'e's in the buildin' game.
'e scorted off by car - an' then -
On seein' me - 'e reverses smartly back -
A sayin,' as 'ow 'e can't stop
Cos 'e's a feared 'e'll get the sack."

I sez I won't stand in 'is way
As 'is drivin' it be bad.
Though 'e did not agree with me, 'e did admit –
'is drivin' 'ad bin (sometimes) described as mad.
'e went on t' say there was some old bloke
Stood over in the pub – who 'ad a photograph
Which 'e'd brought in with 'im –
For me - that was nearly tor' in half.

Well I makes me way across to the pub
Where I sees young Willie Payne
Who sez, "You've come in so late -
I thought as 'ow – you'd forgot again.
"I'm 'ere t' view this ol' picture."
I sez, "So let me see these 'ere 'ome guard."
Which young Willie then passes to me –
Stuck on a piece of ink stained card.

I asks 'im who be they? – To which 'e replied.
"Why – they'm Yubberton an' Paxford's Home Guard.
"No no," sez I, "Do you know any of their names?"
"Well," sez 'e, without me glasses on - I finds it proper 'ard."
"So! Why haven't you got 'em on?" I asked.
"Cos Keener's borrered 'em - so 'e can see where 'e 'as been."
Sez Will, as Keener 'ands 'em back again -
A sayin' as 'ow them glasses needs a clean.

Once bespectacled young Willie takes a look
An' then sez, "Though this picture it be bad
I can see ol' Bunter Beasley
An' the feller one to the left of 'im – well that man - he be me dad.
Then Keener sez "I can't see the Paxford postmaster
Cos the picture isn't very large –
But I knows 'e must be on there
Cos 'e was the (self appointed) Officer-in-Charge.

Well I'd soon 'ad enough o' them
So I takes the photo up to Joy of sewin' -
Well she be a Yubberton lass
An' a girl I trusts as bein' very knowin'
Now straight away she spots 'er dad
An' then quickly names two of the others -
Then runs out of more ideas - but sez,
"Don't worry, I'll take the photo round t' show me mother."

Joy's mother was so very keen
But 'er memory it 'ad gone
An' I don't think she would've recognized
A one – even with young Willie's glasses on.
So Joy returns the photo
With just 'er dad an' the Paxford undertaker
Marked – though she did say
As how Bunt Beasley - once worked - for the Paxford baker.

My last call was to Peter Bocock
Who 'ad been in the Yubberton Guard -
Till he became a 'D' day 'ero
With the regulars - where 'e'd got proper scarred.
'e was keen to take a look
An' remembered several folks
But 'e couldn't name a lot of 'em -
A mutterin' that, "They was familiar lookin' blokes."

Well! Between 'em they 'ave named
A lot more men than 'alf –
Which I pointed out t' Willie
When I 'anded back 'is photograph –
As well as makin' clear
That there was a lot more namin' there t' do -
T' which 'e replied, "I could 'ave named
A lot more of 'em - if I'd really wanted to."

Yubberton's Engineers

My Sunday amblings took me
Along the 'idecote road
Where it was becomin' clear
Much barley 'ad bin sowed.
Then, on turnin' me gaze ahead
A slight movement I could see
There was three ol' men
A walkin' slow in front o' me.

Them ol' boys was known t' me
As Rusty, Tot an' Geof
Them a bein' bald, short sighted
An' very often deaf.
I'd known 'em man an' boy
For sixty years or more
We'd roamed around these lanes
Since, well before the war.

So I would catch up with 'em
By a climbin' on me bike
An' a pushin' they pedals round
At gret speed - or summut like.
I was quickly bearin' down on 'em
When I felt a spot 'o rain
Which I was still a cursin'
When me chain come off again.

Finally I caught up to 'em
An' bade a bright hello
Then was taken by surprise
When told just where I ought t' go.
Well Ol' Totty was a moanin'
You should a 'eard 'im gripe
'ed bin to Paxford shoppin'
Where 'e'd gone an' lost 'is pipe.

Now I'd 'eard 'em once described
As - three motor engineers.
The tall chap was the one
With most between 'is ears,
Another as the fiddlin' one
In a local country band
The third a sportin' Toby jug
With a golf club in 'is 'and.

Just then we met Dougie Cupper
Who 'adn't gone to far
For 'is motorbike 'ad parted
From a newly bought sidecar.
Totty 'ad about 'im
A catgut fiddle string
Which 'e 'anded on to Rusty
A sayin' "This'll fix the thing".

Then Geof took off upon the bike
With Totty in the chair
Leavin' poor ol' Rusty
To sort out the cost of their repair.
'E decided that the fee would be
A roll of solderin' wire
An antique left 'and niblick
An' a pipe made out of brier.

Dougie was most grateful
But asked for time to pay.
Rusty nodded in agreement
Sayin' that 'e 'ad till Lady Day.
Doug looked a bit perplexed
For 'e'd never 'eard of such an 'ummon.
Rusty reassured 'im not to fret
For they 'ad not a lot in common.

The bike an' men did not return
Though there was a rumour came
That ol' Geof 'e was a racin' it
Somewhere out in Spain.
So beware of any three ol' men
For the village 'as it's fears
There's some may lay false claim -
As to bein' - Yubberton's Engineers.

The Yubberton Bus

As I come from out of our Town 'all
I saw young Brian Wheatcroft – stood
'e seemed to be a frettin - so I spoke
In a way I thought would do some good.
"What be the matter Brian?" sez I
'e replies, "I've missed the Yubberton bus."
It's departure time be twelve - now tis 'alf past -
But the last thing I wants is to create a gret big fuss."

"Well," sez I, "I will try an' 'elp you
Cus I knows a thing or two.
It's alus best to ask a local when
You'm lost - an' don't know what to do."
Well Brian thanked me very kindly
Sayin' 'e was sorry that 'e'd swore.
But I re-assured 'im that there was nothin'
In 'is language – that I'd not 'eard before.

Then luck backed up me promise
To transport 'im out of Campden's throng
When – just at that same moment
Ol' Totty and his bwoy (Vince) come along –
A ridin' in from Yubberton
To buy some weekend grub -
All regal like - in their Datsun mini-bus -
An' with good intentions - of a stayin' out the pub.

I must stop 'em both - as they'm a travellin' by
So I steps out - (a wavin' me brightly coloured pullover)
Not such a well thought out manoeuvre –
'cause them lads come near - to runnin' me right over.
But only a few folk was alerted to the screachin'
Of the tyres an' the smoke from off the brakes –
That pulled Ol' Totty up quite short -
Which was a good job - for both of our sakes.

"Can you take young Brian 'ome." Sez I,
"For 'e's gone an' missed the bus."
Ol' Totty sez, "We 'aven't got much room
But 'e's welcome t' 'ave a ride with us."
By now the traffics a buildin' up
An' some driver's are a beginin' t' cus -
Makin' Brian reluctant to walk into the road -
In case 'e should get drawn - into the growin' fuss.
"Quick Brian - the lads 'ave made room for you
So you'll 'ave no trouble a gettin' in
They've stacked their groceries 'igh
So you can sit - on that drum of pink paraffin."
I urges 'im t' run -
With 'is bad knees and dodgy 'ip
A prayin' that no cars bumps into 'im –
An' that 'e doesn't slip – nor trip.

Ol' Totty's lad says, "Dad –
I've 'ad a bright Idea – this one's really good -
We should start our own transport service
It'd be a gret success – I just knows it would –
'specially for carrying folk like Brian
After all - 'e be one of us -
We could go on the local radio
As a new business venture – called - Ol' Totty's Yubberton Bus."

"You can drive 'er daily round an' round -
From Charringworth as far as Ilmington Down -
Through Paxford an' out t' 'idecote
An then – (at weekends) - t' all parts o' Campden Town -
We'll form a limited Company
With the two directors bein' you an' me -
An then - when you gets your bus pass -
You'll be allowed to travel - absolutely free.

Ol' Totty thought long an' 'ard
About Vince's well appointed plan -
Then finally he raised 'is 'ead an' said,
"Son - I'm sorry but I am not your man -
It's not that I minds a gooin'all the way t' Paxford
T' fetch the likes of Keener an' Willie Paine -
It's just that if they found out about me bus pass -
I'd never get over the shame."

Yubberton's Retired Engineer

Ol' Totty is much better now
Since they cut some of 'is bowel away –
'e's back to playin' on the fiddle -
But sez Morris dancin's - for another day.
'e sez that though the tunes be good
'e can't wave about - 'is 'ankerchief -
Cos 'e sez it 'as endured -
A fair amount of snot relief.

'e now spends 'is time a sleepin'
Or takin' breakfast at 'is ease.
'e likes 'is toast with 'oney on
An' sez 'e might take up keepin' bees.
Or otherwise 'e's in the green'ouse
So it's as Ruby's often said,
"Now that 'e's retired - 'e only moves
Between 'is bed an' 'is well glazed garden shed."

'e sez, "With all this glass in
An' all me engineerin' stuff
I can see t' light me pipe with ease
An' do me work up - well enough.
That 'eart attack – (though not real)
Was sent as a timely life reminder
Not t' get too enthusiastic -
When a workin' on the lathe or grinder.

’e sez. “I’ve told ol’ Rust an’ Geoff
Just what it is that they must do –
They must give up all ideas of work
An’ take up retirement too –
Cos it ’elps with your rheumatics
An’ frees up your achin’ joints –
An’ when you goes round to the doctors
You gets more lifestyle points.”

Ol’ Tot ’as always ’ated supermarkets -
Just their mention makes ’im groan
’Cos ’e sez we should all keep pigs
An’ as for veg – well - we should grow our own.
But now every Thursday (middle mornin’)
’e goes where all the rest goes –
With Ruby an’ both ’is terrier dogs -
For shoppin’ - an’ ’is lunch - in Tesco’s.

Cold is the Dusk

Trudging, under navy skies,
Over landscape of a winter's guise,
Lighted only by a pallid sun
Set low, as early evening's done.
The hills inclined from dip to scarp,
The frost increased from rime to sharp
And leafless trees in purple bark
Stand waiting for the coming dark.

Such a scene sets this length of way
For the many coated tramp asway.
Sallow skinned and un-replete
From frosted nose to frozen feet,
His soles are worn, 'neath uppers holed,
Unable now, to stop the bitter cold
And laced to limbs that pain to bend,
As slow they trudge to journey's end.

Each pace rolls from heel to toe
Echoing below the roosting crow,
Tramping down the empty husk
Slower now in gathering dusk.
Hedgerow's long-shed, dying leaves,
Blown by gusty bitter thieves,
Into piles - ripped and torn apart
Like ever-changing modern art.

Full fallen is the freezing night
Her blanket blacking all from sight.
Hidden now, the stiffly fallen leaves
And their divested parent trees,
Impressive guards they stand by day,
But darkness conjures them away,
Replaced by those whose nocturnal cause
Is to hunt their prey with little pause.

The night brings on more change,
With old dog fox, in vest of mange,
Mindful of the badger's swinging claw
Whilst holding distance from his jaw.
Voles alert through dead of night,
To the barn owl's noiseless flight
And insects scavenge every kind,
Of scattered debris left behind.

Good conscience should not allow
A 'down and out' lost to the bough.
But morning light shows the ward
Has found the traveller still abroad
Abandoned to a fearful fate -
Spiked and clemmed by churchyard gate
For want of charity - gone unfound
Within the bounds of holy ground.

Who Stole my World?

Who took my world and filled it up
With such a flood of four-wheel drive cars?
Who took our local pubs
And turned them into trendy bars?
Who planned my house invasion
With television's so called stars -
Who put our fruit in cans
And threw away our bottling jars?

Who took away my boyhood
And made me earn a wage?
Who tore my dreams away from me
To leave me - blank of page?
Whose inconsideration
Pushed those infirm with age -
Out from family home -
And abandoned to 'care' home rage?

Who caught my breath
With rampant lymphocytes -
Charged to turn my ignition off
And put out my navigation lights?
Who tampered with my food
By polluting several bites?
Who's trying to gag my voice
And dull my human rights?

I blame those sound bite politicians -
A cabinet full of 'sin well gents'
Bound up in their correctness
And ill-advised - false intelligence.
Formed in order to carry out their plan
And grab - with mortal implications -
Oil rich Arab lands -
With (their version of approval)
From - our United Nations.

I am perfectly aware that politicians
Didn't make me ill
But there increasing interference
Has fettered my well honed will -
Through which I think and feel
So because of this I think that by and large -
I'm satisfied to see them branded culpable
And - therefore - guilty of the charge.